Heard at a UTAH Diner

A Short Stack of Humor <u>beyond</u> Green Jell-O® and Sister Wives

Gathered by

Steve Odenthal & James D Beers

OdieGroup Press

DEDICATION

This first collection of the humor of Utah is dedicated to everyone who has heard one too many jokes about the desert state and the peculiar people who live here. When I first arrived to attend Weber State University, I had my own questions about this place, and now, forty years later, I proudly still call the state my home. Humor abounds here, it just doesn't manifest itself in ways that get much airtime, and like most anywhere else, the best stories are retold within small communities from one friend to another. A local gathering place like a diner is the natural setting for these exchanges, and that is what James and I have tried to capture for you—a bit of the rural charm of Utah. This anthology offers a sampling of humorists both veteran and new for your enjoyment. And just like the state of Utah, we believe there is something here for everyone. Enjoy.

FOREWORD

Welcome to the first annual anthology of Utah Humor! It has been our distinct pleasure to gather these stories that are meant to amuse and tell about this desert state we call Utah. We hope to bring a few new authors to your attention and give a glimpse into the peculiarities of our culture—all the while keeping you smiling as you read.

We found the type of stories that you might hear in a local diner where friends and family gather and trade these tales. Some are tender, some have a deeper meaning, but all use a voice directly to the reader, as if in a conversation for two. That is the intent of the humorists—to spend time with you. That is why often these stories move from active to passive voice and back again. That switch is often the design when presented publicly. We hope that you will find something here that you like and a new author or two to follow.

Steve & James

Table of Contents

JEREMY & JENNIFER
JENSEN

HOPE YOU GET A LAUGH
OR TWO!
YOUR FAMILY MAKES US
SMILE

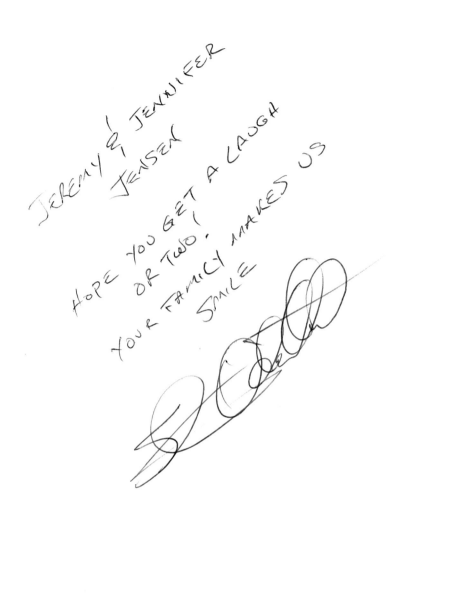

ACKNOWLEDGMENTS

A project like this one is not pulled together without great help from many people. James and I would like to give our thanks to the Humorists that stepped forward from the shadows to share their work with you. Who would have thought that a simple conversation where we looked at each other and speculated, "There must be more like us out there" would result in a collection of fine and thoughtful essays with a humorous twist? Who would have also thought that our good wives, Valerie and Jenna, knowing us as they do, would have allowed us to seek out other writers who were afflicted with the humor gene? They did, so here we are.

Many thanks to our contributing Humorists: Alice M Batzel, Betti Avari, Cecelie Costley, Dave Willes, J Audrey Hammer, Jared Quan, John M Olsen, Josie Hulme, Kathy Davidson, Mike Nelson, and Tyler Brian Nelson—who might have snuck in a horror story on us.

And a special thanks needs to go to James D Beers for being the best co-conspirator I possibly could have had in this undertaking.

Steve Odenthal

The Grass Is Always Greener Where the Sidewalk Ends
Steve Odenthal

There is a parade of sorts each year in Brigham City, Utah—my hometown. Every time it passes by during the UEA school break, I try to watch. It warms my heart and gently reminds me of the innocent time of my youth. Now for those of you unfamiliar with the term UEA, it stands for Utah Educators Association and each year they set the youth of our state free for a couple of days at the end of October so that their membership (teachers and administrators) can congregate in one place to receive career training and guidance. Depending on the individuals involved, this needed off-site assembly can take place anywhere between Salt Lake City to the north, and Disneyland to the south. Usually, a good time is had by all, especially the kids who get Thursday AND Friday off of school. What a good time for a Parade, right? Someone put those two things together 70 years ago and came up with a winner. But this procession is unusual in that it slowly winds through the residential parts of the town rather than re-tracing the downtown route used by our *real* annual parade.

Make no mistake; this annual trek is very much a real and anticipated ritual for our town. Children and parents line the sidewalks, eagerly hoping to be the first to spot the Highway Patrol cars, with their flashing red and blue lights strobing through the normally quiet neighborhoods, as the Troopers and local law enforcement personnel escort a wild and wooly mob through our peaceful town. But like any mob worth it's salt, this flock of twenty-two hundred strong does have a handful of black sheep scattered amongst them. However, even those few seem to be on their best behavior as this group of fluffy whites solemnly troop by my home. These would-be mattress workers file by quietly, as the children call to them from the sidewalk trying to start a conversation. Most in the gypsy herd know that they are merely traveling through, so they do not attempt to engage with the crowd, except for the occasional *baa* here and there. When the woolies reach my block, they become eerily quiet, perhaps silently hoping to avoid the next leg of their journey which will lead them on Watery Lane and past Price's Premium Meats, a place where none of the weary travelers wish to spend any extended time. I can't be sure, but I believe they tip-toe as they pass.

I find it relaxing to see well-controlled livestock on the move--especially if I am not the one moving the herd. I enjoy the simplicity of a seasoned shepherd and a dog leading the flock to the western winter pastures on an established drive-route that has been the trail for more than 70 years. Except for the houses, spectators, cars, and asphalt roads now in place, the route has remained the same, albeit a bit less dusty, for all that time.

Progress can be a good thing, but I much prefer a well-kept tradition. We have exactly that here—a traditional sheep drive. Life in a small town does have its rewards. I am so glad that we haven't given in and tried to enhance our traditions like so many other places do. Other places and civic leaders might propose loading the sheep into trucks and then making this annual ritual more exciting by changing to a Pamplona-style Running of the Bulls down our local streets. Heck, today, even bigger, bolder cities might suggest an exotic spin and substitute rhinos instead of sheep for an additional adrenal rush. Commercially, such a thing might be a success. Out-of-towners would certainly flock in and spend big bucks here to see that sort of spectacle, but you couldn't buy me enough car insurance to make rhinos worth my while. (I park on the street.) And the nice thing is it is just not going to happen here. We tend to be a quiet flock of citizens by nature.

The longer I live here in Brigham City, with its 25,000 citizens, the more I understand that it's good to live in a small town with all of our local traditions. I'll be watching this one with my grandchildren again this year. If I don't see you there, I'll offer a *baa* to a traveling woolie for you.

To Woo or Not to Woo? Dancing Begs the Question

James D Beers

When I was young, I did not know that one day I would like girls. I might have suspected such, given that my dad liked my mom, but in the mind of a prepubescent kid, parental romance is disgusting, even more disgusting than playground crushes. Gross!

At least that's what I thought at the time. Eventually, in my late-preteen to mid-teen years, girls started to look pretty and beautiful and gorgeous and all those other sappy words I couldn't previously coax my tongue to pronounce. I remember thinking, what is the matter with me?! Girls are the enemy! The destroyers of recess football games, trespassers in forts, and wearers of weird things like pantyhose and perfume. And all they want to do is kiss and stuff! UGH!!!

Such was my misguided perception in those transition days to manhood. It didn't help that I was a regular attendant of the under-the-jungle-gym congregation meetings sporadically held on the Grace and Hope Elementary school grounds.

In that solemn group, embellished tall tales about girl cooties and lipstick and mascara were preached by serious-toned boys. Victims of kiss tag told war stories about being held down and cheek-pecked by girls in past recesses.

I once delivered a sermon to a bug-eyed crowd of boys on the dangers of girl herds, relating the time I'd been trampled in a girl stampede. My poor first-grade self haplessly walked into the path of fifteen or so girls in hot pursuit of a fleeing boy, the unfortunate target in a deadly game of catch-and-kiss.

That particular sermon was one of the few crowning moments I had in the limelight of the small gathering. As was custom with great lectures in our group, my delivered address was marked with the approving shouts of "True!" and "Dude!" followed by sympathetic pats on my back from many of the congregation's members. The speech, however, was also the last one I ever delivered to the congregation.

As if Nature herself had flipped a switch and shooed me out, I left the group about the time I turned twelve years old, overtaken by a sudden desire to not run so fast from pursuing girl herds. I wasn't certain what had happened to me until puberty was explained nearly a year later in an atrociously awkward fifty-minute period of seventh-grade health class. Never was there a life period of more confusion! My interest in girls grew, but the onset of pimples, body odor, cracking voice, and hair erupting in bizarre places during what was supposed to be a heaven-sanctioned physical change to manhood killed any confidence I might have had in the presence of my female contemporaries. It seemed a cruel and unusual punishment that I was surrounded by girls eight hours a day, five days a week while my body was turning into a stinky, pimply Sasquatch.

And the conflict between my self-confidence and waxing attraction to girls only got worse.

✱✱✱

Before I sink deeper into this woeful tale, I need to explain something. From what you've read thus far it would seem that I was a girl fanatic. That would be stretching the truth well beyond believability. Yes, I liked girls, but I was also scared to death of them.

As a preteen and teen, I spent my time in the woods, hunting, and fishing, getting dirty, jumping cricks (yes, we called creeks cricks), and playing with sticks and pocketknives. Girls spent their time in malls, sniffing out perfumes, buying nice clothes, and giggling together in large herds.

I often wondered who these peculiar female creatures were and why was I compelled to seek them. The dichotomy was terrifying and broad as an ocean. I was sorely bewildered. Perhaps that was the crux of the dilemma; on the one hand, I was scared to death of girls and not confident in my girl-attracting abilities as a stinky, pimply Sasquatch, while on the other hand I liked girls and planned on having a few dozen girlfriends and marrying one someday.

Despite the fact that my naiveté was thicker than set concrete and that I might have cleared up some misconceptions by talking to my parents, the fear was real and had a firm grip on me. The only way I could confidently face a girl in those days was in a merciless game of dodgeball during PE, and then only if I didn't get too close.

Nothing about girls, however, scared me more than their penchant for dancing. To sappy love songs! With boys! Dancing, other than perhaps a masculine, Sioux war dance, never appealed to me. I'd seen dancing done in movies and on episodes of Buck Rogers and Fantasy Island. With the sound muted, it looked like a bunch of weirdos in a fit of convulsions. Even with the sound on, I couldn't abide the strangeness of gyrating bodies. As far as I was concerned, it was a totally unnecessary human love ritual.

Those were just some of the fearful preteen and early-teen thoughts I had about dancing with girls. And I hadn't even made it to the actual act of dancing.

✳✳✳

Leave it to my parents to create an even greater nightmare for me. At fourteen, they forced me to go to my first church dance. "Look, I'd rather face bears or swim bleeding through a school of piranhas than go to the dance!" I told them.

They cast unsympathetic looks at me, and Dad, with the same tone parents use to tell their kids to eat their vegetables, said, "You're going. Besides, it'll be good for you."

The only thing I imagined it would be good for was giving me clinical anxiety and premature heart failure. I begged and pleaded not to go but to no avail. Despite my fear, somewhere deep in my psyche, a part of me knew that to win over a girl's affections I'd eventually have to learn to dance and then actually dance with a real girl.

But at fourteen, that thought was WAY deep down in the psyche. To say that I wanted nothing more than to be a wallflower at that first dance doesn't come close to an adequate expression. I tried to hide in bathrooms and behind foyer curtains, but a middle-aged lady carrying a baby kept finding me and forcing me back into the church gymnasium where the other teens were wiggling about to eighties and nineties pop and love songs.

"Get back in the action!" she'd say, and I'd mope my way back in there until I could escape again.

The same lady kept telling me the same thing for the next four years of forced church dance attendance. The turmoil and torment I endured left me the psychological equivalent of a pile of mashed potatoes.

Church dances weren't the only problem, either. At seventeen, I was coaxed onto the Junior/Senior Prom Decorating Committee and tricked into staying for the dance. I got so nervous I contracted a blotchy rash that lasted for three months. It ruined my final soccer season and cost me a small fortune in cortisone creams.

✳✳✳

I suppose the dance experiences weren't all bad, but darn close. Eventually, I learned the rock-back-and-forth slow dance, but that was the extent of my learning. My hope was that the dance craze would wear off in college, that it would turn out to be just a teen fad. Boy, was I wrong. Dances were everywhere! I swear the college had one every weekend, sponsored by a different organization each time. There was even a dance club in town where college kids actually paid money to go and dance.

What's worse, I actually went to some of those dances. Of my own volition! I was actively trying to overcome my fear of dancing and girls. In fact, my first date was to a dance with Belinda Spooner. How you might ask, did such a suave, debonair, ladies' man like me never go on a date before college? That's easy. I was chicken.

The dance date idea was concocted by my roommate and long-time friend, Hank Greiney. I've recounted the date before but failed to mention the style with which I "got jiggy with it." Should an octopus stick one of its tentacles in a light socket, the resulting eight-armed spasms would be more rhythmic than the moves I displayed on that first date. It was weird. Heck, I was weird. But I was also determined. Women would see me dance, dang it!

During my second semester of college, I enrolled in Social Dance 101. On the first day of class, I so flustered my dance partner that she stopped our attempted waltz and asked, "Do you know what you're doing?" "Nope. Not a clue," I truthfully told her and then continued waltzing all over her feet. By the time the second day of class rolled around, I had grown so nervous that I began sweating profusely, and my breath took on the acrid aroma of a sour stomach. As the classes continued, I tried wearing black shirts and white shirts to hide the sweat. I layered on the deodorant like frosting on a cake. I chewed minty gums—three pieces at a time! —and sucked on breath mints until I feared I'd lapse into a diabetic coma.

Algebra, biology, art history, Spanish, English composition—all the other classes I took couldn't hold a candle to the anxiety dance class caused me. For as difficult as it was, Social Dance 101 might as well have been graduate-level quantum physics. Nightmares ensued, as did occasional bouts of torrential diarrhea. Like a biblical prophecy, I could foresee a big fat F appearing next to Social Dance 101 on my college report card. I was certain I'd eventually become a dance floor nemesis, averted by all females. Thus, six classes in, I gave up and dropped the course, claiming my sanity and the sanity of my dance partners was at stake. The instructor, plainly aware of my classroom performance, signed the dismissal form without question.

✳✳✳

Such was the end of the first stage in my girl pursuit and dance career. Some might say it was an omen of things to come. To be sure, there were many dating and dancing misadventures that followed. Yet here I am, a married man. How did I ever find a girl and get married, you ask? You might find this hard to believe, but I eventually learned to dance. The salsa, as a matter of fact. One of the things that attracted my wife? My dance moves, particularly my sexy Spanish hips. Ay yai yai!

Providence Canyon

John M Olsen

Having spent my first dozen years growing up near Providence Canyon in Cache Valley, Utah, I can state first-hand that its beauty in winter is legendary. At least at normal speeds.

I'm not talking about motor vehicles. You don't drive that canyon fast in the winter unless you want to fetch a neighbor to winch your truck out of a streambed. No, there was a trick to seeing the canyon at extraordinary speeds. Things always look different when you view it at high speed from less than a foot above the snowpack. You see, the canyon was the ultimate dream as a sled run.

Olympic bobsledders may have beat us for sheer speed, but we had scenery to die for in the rugged canyon with its steep, forested walls interrupted with occasional flat pastures filled with pristine snow.

The large dump trucks from the rock quarry didn't run once the snows came. The job of breaking the trail up the canyon was left to snowmobiles, but once the snow was packed, almost everyone in town had a four-wheel drive truck or Jeep, and chains for the tires if needed. The snow on the packed road was an open invitation to anyone with a Flexible-Flyer sled. All we had to do as kids too young to drive was convince someone to haul us to the top of the canyon, and we could get at least half-way home on our own.

The call came one Saturday morning. My cousin, Mitchell, told me his brothers had the truck ready for a trip to the top of the canyon and asked if I wanted to come along. There's only one answer to a question like that. I bundled up and piled into the truck with them for an adventure.

The canyon seemed longer than normal as we drove up the winding path left by snowmobiles. The snow slowed our pace as we climbed, turn after turn until we finally came to a stop near the top of the canyon, as far as the truck would go. I piled out onto the road with two cousins and one sled for the three of us. We gazed with rapture at the path below us. The canyon spread out below with a breathtaking view reaching all the way out into the valley. The twists, turns, and open flats called to us, promising adventure. We were ready, decked out in enough hats, gloves, and heavy coats to equip a polar explorer's expedition.

My older cousin, Norman, took the bottom position and steering as we formed up into a triple-decker sandwich on the sled. In our young minds, that was more streamlined, and we could go faster than sitting up. I got the middle layer, with my younger cousin Mitchell on top of the stack. We pushed off for our descent.

Wind whipped past as we picked up speed, banking around the first few turns near the top of the canyon. By the time we got to the flats, we sped along fast enough that we barely seemed to slow while crossing between open fields along the packed road. In moments we were through what would have been a calm stretch if not for our speed, and the sides of the canyon closed in once more as we plunged down the canyon. Being on the bottom of our cousin sandwich, Norman also had the job of dragging his feet if we needed to slow down, but he never saw the need as trees flashed by on both sides at an increasing rate, sometimes turning into an evergreen blur.

Now, several decades later, I don't precisely recall all the turns on the way down. It could be I had my eyes closed from time to time to keep the tears from freezing my eyes open as we whipped past trees, rocks, and what may have been the wreckage of less fortunate sled crews.

Adrenaline flowed through me as we tempted fate at what must have been the fastest speed anyone had ever achieved in the canyon. Sleds don't come with speedometers, and it can be challenging to judge such things from ground level, but I'd learned about the space race and how capsules re-entering the atmosphere generated tremendous heat from their speed.

Since I felt nothing but a bone-chilling cold with a threat of frostbite, I knew we were going somewhat slower than astronauts as we whipped through the last few turns and approached the bottom of the canyon where it leveled out into a bench of flat ground for at least a mile before us.

At that point, my eyes cleared of ice and tears long enough for me to see a hundred yards ahead where the snowplows stopped their road-clearing efforts. Our cushion of packed snow and ice gave way to pavement there in the distance, and we still rocketed forward at breakneck speed.

I poked Norman's shoulder and pointed forward. "Road!"

Norman knew his Flexible Flyer at an instinctual level. With the right twists and leans he made it perform maneuvers to boggle the mind, yet he waited as we grew closer to the end of the ice. I continued to poke him and point. I couldn't roll off the sled and leave my cousins to their fate since Mitchel, the top layer of the sandwich, had us all locked to the sled with his vice-like grip.

Finally, Norman pushed the steering as hard as he could and leaned, putting the sled into a sideways slide across what remained of the ice, kicking up a white crystalline plume as we slowed faster than I could have imagined. Just not fast enough.

He'd waited too long, and the sled bit into the road sideways as we made the transition from winter playground to unforgiving pavement.

The resulting mushroom cloud of boys, sled, coats, hats, gloves, and screams was likely visible from space. I flew through the air, seeing the ground, then the sky, then the ground again, my view littered with our flying cloud of debris until everything returned to the ground to bounce and roll.

Our polar expedition coats saved our skins, taking the brunt of the road rash from our rapid stop with only a few small leaks of down feathers as we came to rest, bodies intact. We laughed uncontrollably at the perfection of our sled run.

I have other memories of Providence Canyon, but nothing tops the day I spent with my cousins discovering a new kind of beauty, that of shared memories and laughter. My sledding cousins have both passed on all these years later, but my memory of time spent with them lives on within me, and now, within you.

Tenacious Monkey Bites

Steve Odenthal

I must admit that I am not perfect. Never have been and never will be. But, like all men and perhaps a woman here or there, I have not been exactly energetic in embracing my shortcomings and faults. Some of those shortcomings have been pointed out to me on occasion by a certain loved one who shall remain nameless, because I know that she had only the best of intentions and was, after all, only striving to build a better *me*.

While there could be several adds, moves, and changes in the mix of building a better me, the one item that keeps coming to the top of the list is my ears. Now, I don't want you to jump to the conclusion that I have abnormal, droopy or otherwise unsightly ears – no one is accusing me of impersonating a certain Disney character of the elephantine persuasion, nor do I resemble a certain member of the Royal Family, who might eventually become a king. No. The problem, it seems, is in function, rather than design, of these auditory extremities.

I cannot tell you the number of times my wife has said to me, quite incredulously, "You hear the strangest things!" And you know, I agree with her. I know what I am hearing is strange. Heck. That's why I repeat the words back to her. Even I have trouble believing my ears. I'm just looking for verification that what she said is *really* what she meant.

Usually, when I repeat the offending phrase to the person who first voiced it, the inevitable denial comes. "No, we said *hubcap*, not *Bobcat!*" There is a HUGE difference as to how a driver might react to the word choice here, especially at the end of a twelve-hour marathon drive home, returning from a California vacation.

I know the truth and will take it to my grave. My precious children, whose safety is always my primary concern, had spotted and were excitedly warning me that a bobcat was ahead on the road. Just as those children will forever relive in their dreams the evasive maneuvers I employed to protect them from that wild and hairy threat; no doubt, they also will remember my own high-pitched screams of "Bobcat!? Bobcat!?" to calmly confirm the sighting. Some members of the family will have indelibly etched in their memory the three-sixties and figure-eights performed during said evasive maneuvers. We ALL will remember the innocent hubcap that sprung free from our front tire and rolled harmlessly ahead of our stranded vehicle and out of sight on the highway, continuing its solo journey toward home.

Of course, everyone in the car younger than I insisted that *hubcap* was what they had been screaming all along. Eventually, we drove on. This episode wasn't the first time I acted on some erroneous bit of information—it won't be the last. But there is one time in particular that sticks out in my memory where I still think my ears were *deliberately* led astray, and I followed right behind them.

I was a young father with a beautiful wife and daughter, living the young family's standard life, which, by necessity, included frugality on a major scale. Coupons were clipped religiously, and evenings were spent in simple, enjoyable, and inexpensive pursuits, which quite often included board games. I am not going to brag here, but—wait, yes, I am—I was very, very good at these games. My wife, you ask? Well, she would win on occasion, but I think it tells you something about her plight that she was always on the lookout to find the newest board game available to level the playing field and give her a better chance at beating me. She always seemed to be out for revenge after a game-night loss. Maybe that explains why she sent me on a new game quest the day following one of my more stellar performances. I'll let you judge.

I was at work when the phone on my desk rang. Because I had been well trained as to my duties, I picked up the phone. A sweet voice spoke from the other end, so I instinctively knew that this was not my boss calling. Wait, this might be read in Parowan, so let's say, I knew that the guy who signs my paychecks wasn't on the other end.

"Hey there, can you do me a favor," my wife asks, portraying innocence with every word. "There is a new board-game out at ZCMI. It's a door-crasher special, so I think they are the only place that carries it. I called and asked them to hold one or two of them for us. We're always wondering what to get my parents, so I thought maybe—. They are expecting to sell out, so you need to get down there at lunch today if we hope to get one. Can you get away? You'll like the game."

I chuckled. "Sure, I can get it. I hope that this is one you have a chance of beating me at. Ha, Ha."

It was very quiet for an uncomfortable amount of time on the other end. "Just kidding, dear," I said, knowing that it was too little, too late.

I will now relate to you the rest of the phone call, exactly word-for-word so that you can remain impartial and fair in your judgment.

"You can get it on the second floor over by the puzzles, at the desk."

"Alright, and what is it that I am asking for, exactly?"

"Tenacious Monkey Bites."

"I'm sorry?"

"Tenacious Monkey Bites."

"Did you say, "Tenacious Monkey Bites?"

"Tenacious Monkey Bites! For the third time!" she said with a bit of irritation in her sweet voice.

"Okay – I got it. I guess. We're talking a board-game, right?"

"Yes. It's a board-game. It takes at least two to play."

"Right-O. Anything else I should know?"

"It's based on a book by Chris Heimerdinger."

"By Chris Heim—" I stopped myself because I knew she had made up the name. There was no way I was going to have her say the name again, after how tense she became repeating the title three times. "OK, I've got it – on the second floor, right."

After a few other assignments, the call ended. Now, I knew that she wanted me to use that made-up name, *Chris Heimerwhatever* while I was at the counter in the store, probably to get some form of retaliation for her epic loss in last evening's entertainment. I'm sure she felt that the store clerk's laughter over my mangling of the author's name, even if she were not there to hear it, would be small revenge on me. I pictured my sweet wife chuckling to herself as she imagined the scene. Lunchtime arrived, and I set about my appointed rounds. Serious and on-task best describes my demeanor as I walked up to the steps to the second floor of ZCMI, a store of proper demeanor and fashion that was famous for their unadvertised door-crasher specials. I immediately navigated over to their Puzzle and Game section and started perusing the shelves, searching for a jungle-themed box, which I was sure would contain the game of Tenacious Monkey Bites. I couldn't find it. It wasn't there. Nothing even close. A clerk came by.

"Can I help you find something?"

"I was looking for one of your door-crashers. It's a game with monkeys."

"The Door Crashers are over here in this area, I hope you find it, but we do sell out."

"Well, thanks. I'll find it." I looked and looked. No game, but lots of empty shelves. I was about to give up when I remembered that my wife had told me that the store said they would hold a game for me at the counter—if I got down there today. It was still today, so there was at least a chance!

With a very large smile pasted on my face, I walked confidently over to the counter attended by a charming young lady of; I would guess, eighteen years of age. A short distance off to her right, mingling amongst the merchandise and other customers stood, I noticed, a well-dressed and very observant member of the security staff. (I'm not sure why I can always spot these guys – I just have that knack. It's like we are always visiting the same places at the same times. It's uncanny.)

It was lunchtime, and the second floor was short-staffed. Moe, the security man, was being extra vigilant; I sensed that he had adopted an added protective posture towards this particular register-keeper. I could well understand his manner as she, like the entire female staff of this store, seemed to project youth and innocence not often seen outside of Disney amusement parks.

"I'm here for Tenacious Monkey Bites," I said in what I thought was a normal voice although by the reaction of Moe and a few other shoppers I may have projected a bit more than I intended. In fact, some onlookers later claimed that I had somehow announced my intentions over the store's PA system.

"What was that?" the young clerk asked as her eyes widened, and the smile left her lips. The color drained from her face. I could see Moe move a step or two closer to the counter and start to eye me a bit.

That made me nervous, and my voice cracked a bit as I tried to explain. "I'm on my lunch-break, and my wife sent me here to get a couple Tenacious Monkey Bites. She told me that you would have them for me at the counter."

"I… I would have them, Sir? A monkey bite—for you?" Moe moved a step closer and loosened the front button of his sport-coat. His eyes seem to be somewhat dilated, and he was definitely very interested in this conversation.

"Well, of course, I was hoping for more than one. I know they are in high demand, but if you can only give me one, I'll be happy."

"I'll bet you would," Moe interjected sternly. I could see Moe was getting somewhat agitated, so I tried to choose my words carefully.

"It's a game – it takes two to play?"

"Oh, this isn't a game. And there is no one playing here."

"We don't have that game, Sir. I think you're mistaken." The clerk managed to squeak out.

"But my wife called earlier—" I was really very nervous about Moe's intensity, so I figured I would ease the tension with the made-up name my wife had given me. Sure, I might look foolish, but a laugh, even at my own expense, would cool things down. And who knew maybe it would be close enough to give them a clue so we could all be on the same page.

"It's by a guy named Chris... Heimer...Dinger?"

Moe had heard enough. "Alright, Sir. I'm going to have to ask you to step away from the counter." He wasn't laughing. The young lady at the counter looked stunned for a few seconds and then smiled brightly.

"What was that name?" "Chris… Heimerdinger?" I replied meekly as Moe started some type of chiropractic therapy on my arm that had me dancing in place on my tiptoes. Moe then took me by the elbow, and we were about to depart to pretty much wherever he had in mind.

"Oh! You mean *Tennis Shoes Among the Nephites*!" The young clerk's attitude seemed greatly relieved.

"I guess! That certainly could be it. But I was pretty sure it had a monkey in it."

Moe slowly eased his grip and then grabbed one of the door-crasher games from a shelf behind the counter. He quickly looked at the box. "No monkey in this one! But I'm pretty sure it's the game you're leaving with." Looking at the box, Moe read to me. "Hours of enjoyment. *Enjoy*. Pay the lady."

This might be the proper time to tell you that there is, indeed, an author by the name of Chris Heimerdinger and that there also is a board-game based on his series of novels, *Tennis Shoes Among the Nephites*. And, yes, it was a door-crasher special on this day at ZCMI. But I would like you also to note – there is *not* a monkey to be found on that box. As Moe and I left the store together, I would love to tell you that he and I struck up a long-term friendship, but alas, it was not to be. I went my way, and he went his, both of us kind of curious as to what had transpired in the store that day.

When I arrived home that night, I was welcomed with a wonderful pot roast dinner and a couple of bright smiles from my wife and daughter. I had decided to not trouble anyone with a recounting of the events of the day.

But I did mention, "Say, I got that game today. You know the one you wanted. *Tennis Shoes Among the Nephites*—that was the name, wasn't it?"

"Oh. Yes, that was it. Was it hard to find?"

"No, it was at the counter. Met a nice man named Moe who hustled me right through."

"Oh. Good. Glad, you didn't have any trouble." I sensed the hint of a giggle in her voice. My wife seemed extraordinarily happy and generally in great spirits throughout the meal. When dinner was over, dishes done, and daughter to bed, I prepared the table for our new board-game and the challenge that is game night. As my wife joined me at the table, she seemed to be very pleased with herself – almost as though she had somehow already won the game. I handed her the unopened box. She looked it over very carefully, noting every detail, then handed it back.

"That's very strange," She said.

"What's strange?"

"I thought it would have a monkey on the box, that's all, dear."

Brigham City Sunshine and Moonshine

Betti Avari

S wish, swish, slice! Scoop. Stuff, stuff.
    "Davey, stop climbing on the furniture."
    "Uh-uh!"
"Davey..." Mom sighs. "Please go play outside."
"But it's hot outside!" Davey growls.

I shoot him a dirty look. We grownups are busy canning peaches and have no time for distractions. If we get all of our canning done today, Mom promised we could go to Crystal Hot Springs tomorrow. Swish, swish, slice! Scoop. Stuff, stuff.

Ignored, Davey jumps from the window seat. "Moooooommmm!" He wraps his arms around Mom's waist and gives her a tight bearhug.

"Oof!" Mom wipes her hands on her apron and turns to face her perpetually forgotten middle child. "Too hot, you say? If you ask me, it feels much nicer in Brigham City, than it does back home in St. George. Don't you think, Hazel?"

"Oh, yeah!" I sigh and wipe my forehead on my sleeve. "Outside," I qualify, "it probably feels fabulous."

"Doesn't feel different to me," Davey mopes.

I roll my eyes. Back home, it's hot enough to fry bacon on the sidewalks. Meanwhile, Northern Utah is much cooler, so we head upstate to Grandma Gwen's house for a few weeks every summer. Ironically, our timing always coincides with the peach harvest, which means there's loads of canning to be done—in a hot kitchen. But Grandma's basement has cool cement floors and a cellar that is cooler still, and that's something St. George doesn't have. When I'm finished helping, I'll take my book and lie down on that floor to cool off. If Davey knew what was good for him, he'd do just that. But he's too dumb to see reason, and he's gonna let the whole household know about it.

Mom's still patiently working with him. "If that's the case, I can put you to work…C'mon, Davey. Tell me, does it feel better outside?"

He looks down at his worn sneakers. "Yeah."

"Well then, young man? Head on outside this very minute." Beside me, Uncle Jack continues pitting and slicing the peaches I put in his bowl, but with Mom distracted, the bowl's filling up. I slow down; Uncle Jack gets stressed out when he's behind. And they don't trust me with a knife yet.

"But there's no one to play with!"

"Mikey's playing in the irrigation trough with Grandpa," Mom suggests.

"Mikey's just a baby."

Mom's exasperated sigh is lost on Davey. "Then play with Cousin Alan and Cousin Roger!" He begins to pout, and Mom finally puts her foot down. "David Andrew Winterton, we've got two more bushels of peaches to finish canning before we can begin to think about dinner, so you best get on outside and stop pestering us, or you'll go to bed hungry."

"Yes, ma'am."

Davey's quiet for a long moment. Mom gets back to work, doing her best to ignore him entirely. Swish, swish, slice! Scoop. Stuff, stuff. Out of the corner of my eye, I watch Davey steal a handful of peach pits out of Uncle Jack's bowl, but I say nothing. I know Alan and Roger are up the tallest tree in the orchard, making a fort Davey isn't brave enough to climb to, but are they out of throwing range? Down the back stairs, I hear the screen door slam.

I scoot so Uncle Jack can reach into the sink. He cleans out the peach skins, and I look behind him, toward the wall beside the fridge, where the two wooden bushels brimming with peaches still await their spa treatments. It's going to be a very long, hot day.

Grandma Gwen shuffles into the kitchen from the clothesline in the backyard, carrying her now-empty hamper. She leans over a bowl of peaches beside me and closes her eyes as she takes a whiff. "Ah! Smell that Brigham City Sunshine!"

Uncle Jack chuckles. "It's hard to imagine a cold winter day right now, but someday soon these peaches will be the only bright yellow thing in sight."

I turn to Mom and whisper, "Is that why Grandma calls them that?"

"Mm-hmm. And her mother called them that, and probably her mother."

"All the way back to the pioneers?"

Uncle Jack winks at me. I turn and look at Grandma, who is opening another bucket of sugar beside the dining table. While Grandma's not an actual pioneer, she came from sturdy pioneer stock, and I'd like to think her wrinkles and leathery skin would be at home in a bonnet on a trek across the plains.

"I think it's neat that we still say the same things that our ancestors used to say," Mom muses a little louder. "Don't you, Mama?"

I grin. "Like Grandpa when he says, 'Fiddlesticks!' if something goes wrong?"

Grandma hates it when he says that.

Sure enough, Grandma pipes up. "You'd think your Grandpa would know the first thing about fiddles," she mutters under her breath as she finally pries the lid off the sugar bucket.

Uncle Jack grunts, "Back to work!" and dumps a fresh bushel of peaches into the sink.

A sudden commotion erupts in the backyard, and I'm guessing one of Davey's peach pits found its mark. Grandma places an understanding hand on Mom's and Uncle Jack's shoulders at the kitchen sink. "If you take a peek on the children, I'll tend to the canning."

Mom rolls her eyes with a good-natured smile and follows Uncle Jack outside.

A loud yelp follows. "Davey Wintert—Aah!"

Grandma and I stare at each other for a split second before running to the back window, and we're just in time to watch Mom run through the open screen door and down the stairs. As the door is closing, a peach flies through the opening and down the stairwell.

Splat!

"Mom?" I shout as the door slams shut.

Two more peaches hit the screen door, and an over-ripe one leaves its mark as it clings to the screen, slowly releases, and plops to the cement landing.

I watch Alan and Roger pluck a few peaches from the uppermost limbs of their tree and aim them at Davey, who is standing dangerously close to the fresh clothes hanging on the line. Uncle Jack retrieves and lobs a few back at them playfully.

"Knock that off, you crazy boys," Grandma laughs. "Or I get the feeling that Crystal Hot Springs will be out of the question tomorrow."

Uncle Jack straightens up and does his best to wipe the grin off his face as he motions for the boys to lay low. "Yes, ma'am."

Mom comes up the stairs slowly. A smile spreads across her face as she turns to reveal the large wet mark on the back of her shirt. "If you think this is bad, just know that I'm gonna need a mop downstairs!" she chuckles.

Uncle Jack helps her with the cleanup, and Grandma and I head back to the kitchen. I turn the faucet on once more and pick up the peeler with a smile. I'm not so bored anymore.

Two hours later, every peach is peeled, every jar filled.

What doesn't fit into the jars goes into a pot for pie filling, and Grandma Gwen lets me help make the crust. I set to work cutting shortening into the flour and watch as Grandma adds a teaspoon of cinnamon and a tablespoon of sugar, and winks at me.

"Such a sweet filling needs a pleasant crust to hold it all together, just like your kind heart shines through your pretty face, dear."

I smile.

"But remember," Grandma takes on a serious tone as she reaches for the saltshaker and dashes a little in, "we need to be a little salty to balance out the sweet, or the dish gets boring." She winks at me again and turns back to the stove where she ladles simple syrup into the waiting jars of peaches.

My thoughts turn to our earlier conversation. "Grandma Gwen, did your grandma *really* call peaches 'Brigham City Sunshine'?"

"She *really* did," she chuckles. "I remember the first time I heard the phrase. One night, with a thunderstorm raging overhead, Grandma Ruby saw I was scared, so she reached into her cupboard and brought out a jar. She said she'd been saving a little bit of summer sunshine for just such a storm. I asked her where she got it. 'The peaches caught the sunshine for us in Brigham City,' she told me. 'Then I bottled them up.' I fell asleep at the dining table on that stormy night, watching our Brigham City Sunshine glow in the firelight. When I woke the next morning, I was tucked in bed, and Grandma Ruby was making flapjacks. I came to the table and sat down as she flipped three fluffy flapjacks onto my plate. She finally popped the lid off the bottle of Brigham City Sunshine and spooned some on top of my stack. There I was, excited to taste my own bite of sunshine, when suddenly—Baaaa!"

The sound is so unexpected in the quiet kitchen that I jump, fork in hand, as flour goes flying out of the bowl of pie crust before me.

Then Grandma bursts into laughter. "Oh, blizzard!" she sputters, her face covered in flour. She takes off her glasses, and a ring of flour surrounds her face.

"I'm sorry, Grandma! You scared me!" I gasp.

We laugh and laugh as she wipes her glasses clean.

"Oh, Hazel, I was as scared then as you were just now, with similar results, I might add!"

"Did you throw food at your grandma, too?"

"Close. When I jumped, a slice of peach flew off my fork and landed on the rug—across the room near the fireplace. And a fuzzy little black lamb sitting beside the fire bent down and ate it up."

"So that's what made the noise?"

"Yes, ma'am—the runt of a pair born during the storm the night before. She wouldn't survive the night out in the cold, so Grandpa brought her inside."

"And she ate the peach? I bet she loved it!"

"You know she did. After the lamb ate it, she bellowed again! So, we named her Peach Fuzz."

"Did she make it through the winter?"

"That winter, and much longer still. To a ripe old age. I still have a scarf made from her very own Peach Fuzz wool."

"You do?"

"I'll show you tonight. It's the softest black wool I ever did feel."

The screech of the screen door pulls us from the story. "Mama!" Mom hollers from the backyard. The door slams and Mom comes running up the steps. "Mama, come quick. We need a ladder!"

Though she's covered in flour, Grandma hops up and heads straight for the tool shed. I run after her.

The air really is cooler outside. The entire family is gathered around a peach tree in the center of the orchard. I hop over the irrigation trough and down the path to the tool shed but stop in my tracks.

Stuck high up the tree on a limb, hanging like a peach, is my brother Davey. He's upside down, suspended by a belt loop, and naked to his knees. His shirt is hanging down over his face, and his arms flail every few seconds. He's stuck.

"Give us just a minute, Davey!" Grandma hollers, doing her best to restrain the smile spreading across her face. "We'll pluck you down from there." She props the ladder on the trunk, then steps back and chuckles. "He's hangin', hangin' like a peach!"

Uncle Jack busts out, laughing. "It's attention he wanted, and attention he gets."

"I guess that's one way to cool off!" Mom shakes her head and begins to laugh, too.

Alan and Roger and Grandpa laugh, and finally, I join the rest, but I'm the only one brave enough to say it. Between giggles, I point and exclaim, "Brigham City Moonshine!"

I don't know how long my little brother, Davey "Moonshine" Winterton hangs from that limb before we compose ourselves, but his nickname sticks in our memory for the rest of our lives.

Just like Brigham City Sunshine.

Bee in My Bonnet

James D Beers

Several years ago, not long after I bought my first house in Ogden, Utah, I had the notion of going off the grid, of trying to live without relying on utility companies and grocery stores. At the time, the community was experiencing an upswing in the self-reliance movement. The hype caught my attention, especially since the monthly bills for running a household demanded an amount equivalent to the indentured servitude of not only myself but also my posterity into the next century. Something other than my emaciated wallet had to give. So, I started looking into it.

I read self-reliance books, perused Internet articles on food storage, checked out survivalist stores, planned for a garden, and attended prepper events. Over the short course of a few months, I became an armchair expert on solar ovens, canning tomatoes, when to plant vegetables, water purification, and pooping off the grid.

Now, I know what you're thinking: this guy probably turned his whole yard into a vegetable patch and was probably hoarding food and water in his basement, erecting solar panels and windmills on top of his house, and pooping off the grid in his backyard.

Well, you'd be *mostly* wrong. Yes, I planted a garden, but it was a small affair—only half my yard was dedicated to vegetables, the rest was reserved for fruit and nuts, namely a couple of apple trees, an apricot tree, a rhubarb plant, a raspberry patch, a grapevine, and a walnut tree. And yes, I also built up a fair supply of food and water, but only enough for a year, that's all. As far as windmills and solar panels? Well, they cost lots of money which I didn't have. Also, I couldn't have my neighbors watching me poop off the grid in the backyard. That would be embarrassing, and probably against the law.

Given the relatively meager beginning of my journey off the grid, I decided that my next step would also be small and practical.

I ordered a hive of bees.

Yep, I found a beekeeping supply and bee mail-order company online and put in an order for a beekeeper kit, queen bee, and three pounds of entourage bees.

That's 30,000 to 40,000 live bees!

Pollinating my garden!

Making honey!

Creating a self-reliance haven!

For me!

I imagined tomatoes by the gross drooping from rows and rows of tomato plants. Visions of raspberries the size of golf balls drove me to drool. I pictured corn and green beans so thick I'd have to beg people to take the excess. And the honey! Oh, the honey! Nectar of the gods wouldn't be as sweet. Certainly, I'd make headlines in the city newspaper: Local's Bees Save Gardens, Fruit Trees Across Town! USDA Approves New Super High-Grade Honey from Local's Beehive.

To prepare myself, I borrowed a video on beekeeping from the library. The video's entire thirty minutes was a live demonstration, from getting your bees in the mail to slapping them into a hive box and then making the first hive check. According to the guy on the video, bees were virtually maintenance-free. Basically, all you had to do was dump them in a hive and let them do their business. Ten days after installment, you check the hive to see if everything is A-Okay. I couldn't believe how well my investment was turning out. And the bees hadn't even arrived yet!

✳✳✳

Before I could get too hasty though, there were a couple of things in the video that caused me just a tiny bit of pause. For one thing, when the bees arrived, the video guy went to the post office where a nice mail lady pulled a box of bees out from behind the counter and just handed it to him. Then she waved and smiled as he and the bees left. It seemed all too; I don't know…nonchalant. Then when the video guy returned home, and after he placed the queen in her special little box inside the hive, he just shook out the rest of the 40,000 bees like he was salting a stake. Without getting stung! It couldn't be that easy; it just couldn't! Could it?

Before I could spend a full week properly ruminating over the question, my beekeeper kit arrived, and within a couple of afternoons, I had slapped the hive boxes and frames together and painted the outside of the boxes white. Scarcely had I finished with the kit when the bees arrived. Judging from the phone call I received from a postal worker, I think the post office wasn't as optimistic about beekeeping as I was.

"Mr. Beers?" asked a nervous voice on the other end. In the background, I could hear screaming while someone shouted "Get back! Get back!"

"Yes…" I replied, wary of the frantic voice on the other end. "This is he."

"This is the post office. Come and get your bees NOW!!!" CLANG! The receiver on the other end slammed down, but not before I heard one last scream and a lady yell, "Run!"

When I screeched to a stop at the post office, I found a sign on the front door reading: Mr. Beers, your bees are out back on the loading dock. We left the gate open for you. An arrow on the sign pointed to an open gate on one end of the building. I made my way out back and immediately spotted the package—a hard-to-miss buzzing and writhing clump of bees in a mesh-sided wooden box held together with a handful of staples. A few dozen solo bees flew around the outside of the box, either trying to find their way in or possibly flying patrol should there be any attacks from intruders. My gut reaction was, Holy crap! How am I supposed to get these bees home? But, according to the guy on the video I borrowed from the library, I was just supposed to pick up the box, put it in my car, and take it home with me, like any other passenger. Sure, it sounds nice and easy in the video, but when you're staring at a mess of 40,000 venom-filled insects held in check only by a piece of holey fabric, suddenly the instructions seem lacking in important details.

Additionally, when you get an urgent phone call from the post office as I did, you don't think about grabbing your new mesh bee bonnet or protective gloves before you take off in response. Instead, lawsuits and a whole division of allergic postal workers lying on the floor in anaphylactic shock sprints through your mind as you speed to your destination. Standing there in shorts and a t-shirt, I felt woefully exposed. The part of me that wanted to run whispered, "Hey, why don't you just leave and forget you ever ordered the bees. You can change your phone number and join the witness protection program. No one will ever know."

Just as I was about to take my own advice, a door next to the loading dock opened a crack, and someone yelled out: "Hurry up and take your bees!" Then the door slammed, and an angry face filled in the door's small window, the person's two squinted eyes watching me like a starving-crazed eagle. From the look on the person's face, it was apparent that if I didn't grab my bees and go, there'd be some kind of federal charges and probably prison time. I had no choice; with my butt cheeks clenched in fear, I waddled up to the bee box, picked it up, and waddled back to my car, the solo bees following me in tow.

My frantic drive home was a needless exercise in cutting corners and breaking the speed limit. For all the fear that the bees had caused at the post office, they were the perfectly polite passengers on the way home—no menacing threats buzzed from their mesh prison, no attacks from the solo bees, not even a fluctuation in their constant, low-C drone. It was *exactly* as the guy in the video described. Perhaps the postal workers' fear and my fear was all for naught. Still, there were 40,000 bees squirming around in a flimsy box in my possession. Entangled in my DNA was a primeval alarm screaming "Danger! Danger! Bees sting! Not good!" So, I found it hard to accept the video guy's advice entirely. Besides, videos come from Hollywood, and Hollywood is the least trusted source on the planet, right?

✱✱✱

Dressed in a pair of thrift store overalls and donning my veiled bee bonnet and sting-proof gloves, I paced around the car—the bees still in the passenger seat—waiting for my neighbor Bud Glaspy to show and give me a hand. Bud and his wife Sue were also riding the self-reliance wave, so when I mentioned the bees to him during our weekly game of high-stakes Uno, he insisted on being there to help with the installment.

When I arrived with the bees and called Bud, he said he'd be over in a heartbeat. At only two houses down and after slipping on his overalls, I figured that meant less than ten minutes. Thirty minutes later, Bud arrived sporting a full-body wetsuit and one of those retro diving masks with the big oval face.

"Bud," I said, unable to stop staring at him and his underwater get-up. "We're gonna be in my backyard, not Captain Nemo's Nautilus."

"It's all I had," Bud replied with a pronounced nasally voice, his nose pinched in the face mask. "Do you think the flippers are too much?"

I looked down at the flippers and gave my shoulders an indifferent shrug. "Nah, but you can probably ditch the snorkel. Wouldn't want a bee climbing down in there."

"Right," Bud removed the snorkel, a slight shade of pinkish chagrin glowing through the tempered glass of his facemask. "Okay, let's see these bees of yours."

I pulled the box of writhing and humming insects from the car, holding it at arm's length, still not used to the idea of toting around stinger-equipped bugs. "What do ya…gulp…think?" I asked.

Bud's bug-eyed look stared out of the face mask, and his mouth dropped open wide before he said, "They come like that?"

"Yep! Straight to the post office." I started into the backyard, anxious to get the show on the road. "Let's get these buggers into the hive."

Bud, his flippers clopping on the driveway concrete and then swishing through the lawn, followed me back to the hive I bought and assembled a month prior.

✳✳✳

Opening the bee package felt like arming a nuclear warhead. One nervous jiggle extracting the can of sugar water and the queen and I felt certain a squadron of tiny fighter pilots would explode all over Bud and me. But that's not what happened. In fact, nothing happened; the bees just sat there humming away.

"Geez Bud, this isn't that hard after all," I said, my confidence waxing.

"Yeah! Whoever thought bees were dangerous? That's nuts!"

Once I had the queen's small cage hanging between a couple of hive frames, I dumped the bees into the hive and spread them out with my hand—like butter on toast—so Bud could put the remaining frames in, and I could set the cover and close the hive lid.

With the cover and lid on, I turned to Bud and removed my bee bonnet, no longer concerned about bee stings. "Boy, these bees are as docile as sheep," I said.

"Holy mackerel!" Bud reached to give me a high-five with his neoprene gloved hand. "I never thought it would be that easy."

"Yeah, I thought for sure I'd open the package, and we'd be stung to death—right through our clothes!"

"Crazy, right?" Bud chuckled. "You oughta call the post office and tell 'em they had nothing to worry about."

We stood there laughing and reveling in our flawless bee installation.

"Looks like I'm a real beekeeper now."

"Yeah, congratulations!" Bud gave me a friendly slap on the back, "What's our next step?"

"According to the guy on the video, we wait ten days, and then we open up the hive and give it a look-see, make sure the queen is laying eggs, and the bees are making comb."

"It's a plan then," Bud sounded as excited as I was about beekeeping. "I'll meet you here in another ten days. About what time do you think?"

"Oh, after work, maybe six-thirtyish."

✳✳✳

Over the following ten days, I didn't go anywhere without mentioning my new docile bees. I told the next-door neighbors and also brought it up in a conversation with the checker at the grocery store. When my state beekeeper license arrived in the mail, I framed it and showed my coworkers. I even took some photos and video on my smartphone to show the guys at church.

After just a few days, it seemed the whole neighborhood was abuzz with bee fever. Conversations with neighbors over fences turned into lessons on beekeeping. Friends called me up to see if they could come over and look at my hive. One church lady brought over a half dozen empty honey bear bottles offering to pay me ten bucks a container full of honey. What surprised me the most, however, is when my son Joseph's first-grade teacher called and asked if she could bring the class by to observe the hive and learn about bees from yours truly.

Pretty soon the whole northern section of the town knew about my bees. People I normally only saw in passing stopped to talk bees and honey.

"I hear you got yourself some honeybees."

"How's your hive doing?"

"Is it true that honey is bee spit?"

"Didn't I read somewhere that honey is good for the skin?"

"Did you know that bees can be trained to find land mines? Saw it on a documentary."

News about the hive check also traveled fast. By the time ten days rolled around, checking the bees had turned into an event to rival the county fair. My wife, Jenna, invited the whole church congregation over to watch. She spent the morning of the tenth-day baking bee and beehive-shaped cookies topped with a dab of honey.

"Hey, what are these?" I asked, walking in from work and trying to reach for one before Jenna slapped my hand away.

"Those are for the hive check guests. I'm going to have Joseph dress in a black-and-yellow striped shirt and pass them out while you and Bud examine the hive. It'll be so cute!"

I started to wonder if I'd have to shower and dress up for the event, but it wasn't until Bud came over about a half-hour before our scheduled beehive work that I realized just how big this bee business had gotten.

"I hope you don't mind," Bud said, "but I invited the neighbors and a few relatives over to watch. I told 'em to bring their own chairs."

"Holy mackerel!" I wasn't upset but was certainly surprised. "How many did you invite?"

"I don't know…maybe…fifty or sixty."

"FIFTY OR SIXTY!" I jumped up from the couch where I was sitting and began pacing the living room floor. "If they come and the church comes," I did a quick tally in my head, "that'll be like…150 people! I didn't have that many guests at my wedding! And it was on a Saturday!"

"I also bought twenty packages of hot dogs and buns for everyone who shows up," Bud just kept laying it on, "and was hoping to cook them on your grill."

Before I could shake the shock from my system, I noticed through the living room window that a handful of guys from the church were carrying tables and chairs to my backyard.

"You've gotta be kidding me!" I gawked as table after table and chair after chair was carried past the side of the house. Bud left the piano bench where he'd been sitting and joined me at the window.

"Ooh," Bud remarked, taken aback himself. "Looks like this is turning into a real shindig."

Suddenly nervous, I turned to Bud and said with a sigh, "I guess we better get ready for this…performance. And this time, Bud, I suggest you ditch the diving suit."

✳✳✳

I was sitting at the dining room table tucking my overalls into my boots when Bud burst through the front door wearing blue snow pants tucked into cowboy boots, a purple Weber State University hoodie too broad for his shoulders, and a straw Mexican sombrero draped with military-green mosquito netting. Before I could laugh, he grabbed me by the shoulders and said, "The street is lined with cars—there's not a parking spot left! And your backyard is full of people!"

Quickly I tied my boots and jumped to the dining room window. People were still walking up and down the sidewalk toward my house, some of them carrying trays and bowls of sundry eats. In all my previous years living in various locations across the western United States, I had never lived in a more supportive and generous community. Neighbors left frozen turkeys on doorsteps at Thanksgiving, cookies showed up on birthdays, hot soups came in caring hands when a person was sick, and baby blankets and home-cooked meals were gifted to delivered mothers. And now, it appeared, my little part of town was putting on a potluck at a beehive check!

"D'ya know what this means, Bud?"

"Yeah," Bud said matter-of-factly. "We don't have enough hot dogs."

"No!" My eyes went wide with deeper realization, and I started bouncing up and down. "My bees are famous! It's just like Charlotte's Web!"

"Oh yeah!" Bud started bouncing with me.

"It's Zuckerman's famous pig…only this is Beers's famous bees! They're gonna write stories about this—it'll be in the news!" "It'll go down in history," I exclaimed, "as the first celebrated beehive!"

Before Bud and I could get a hold of ourselves, Jenna and Bud's wife Sue came inside through the kitchen side door.

"Hey, you two!" Jenna said. "Stop dancing around and get out there!"

"People are waiting for you!" Sue chimed in.

Bud and I smoothed down and double-checked our protective layers and then followed our wives outside.

As we passed the back corner of the house and came into view of the gathered crowd, thunderous applause erupted. Both of us stopped and stared over the hordes of people, broad grins splitting our faces. To our left, some old ladies were fussing over a few tables stacked with tubs of baked beans, trays of veggies and dips, bags of rolls, pans of cake, brownies, and cookies, and several containers of the ubiquitous and obligatory green Jell-O salad. Joseph, dressed in his bee motif shirt, was making his way through the throngs, passing out cookies. To our right, in front of the detached garage, the grill was sizzling with hot dogs.

"Milk it," Bud whispered in my ear and then bowed before he started toward the hive, waving at the spectators like a parade beauty queen. I followed suit, waving and smiling as the crowd continued their applause.

Approaching the hive, Bud quieted the audience with the usual hand gestures and then whispered again in my ear, "Give 'em a speech."

Just the word "speech" was enough to give me the heebie-jeebies and spur my gag reflex. I wanted to defer to Bud, but the audience looked at me with heavy anticipation, and I knew I had to take this one. My languid brain, however, would not come to my rescue. It sagged in my skull, whistling a senseless tune as if to say, "I got nothin'." So, I did what I normally do in such situations—I pretend everyone is naked and let my mouth do the talking.

"Hello, and…uh…welcome to our hive check, where…um…all your self-reliance dreams come true."

For several seconds I floundered in silence, lost in the limbo of my stupefied mind. Oh, the things that come out of my mouth, I privately lamented. I seriously wondered how on earth a nervous guy like me ever got married. Then, Bud came to my rescue, coaxing the crowd into rousing applause before addressing them himself.

"Ladies and gentlemen, if you'll please take your seats we will now, without further ado, check the hive."

Bud and I turned to the hive, and Bud removed the lid. Several bees scurried down into the hive through the center hole in the cover. The audience oohed and aahed. I pulled the cover off, and the two of us peered into the wooden box, the hum of thousands of bees meeting us as we stared between the frame slats at the writhing mass.

The brief moment of the bees' docile nature we had experienced ten days prior, passed like steam in the wind. Before we could remove our heads from hovering inches over the frames, the queen sent out the first squadron of her royal air force. The bees had hunkered down and set up defenses. A couple of dozen tiny fighter pilots flew up into our veiled faces and began gnawing at and trying to poke their stingers through the netting. Both of us jerked back in alarm, and the audience gasped.

"Not to be alarmed, folks," Bud assured the onlookers, "we've got this under contr*ooooaaaahhh*!"

Bud had spoken too soon. The second wave of fighter pilots broke out of the hive, one of them stinging Bud on the arm through his hoodie. The crowd gasped again as Bud let out a short yelp.

"It's okay! It's okay!" I heard Bud trying to tell the audience. But if he said anything else, I didn't catch it, for a bee had wriggled its way inside my veil and was buzzing around looking for a tender spot to poke me. Panicked, I began a caffeinated rendition of the Mexican hat dance around Bud and the hive, swatting at my face as if I had it on the ropes and screaming like a horde of schoolgirls at a boy band concert.

"Run James! Run!" I heard Bud's voice through my screams. At the time, I didn't realize how absurd it was to run when the bee was still in my veil. Nonetheless, I plowed over Bud on my way toward the house, still swatting away at my face. But, in my haste to escape, my foot caught and dislodged one of the cinder blocks holding up the hive. The queen's entire fortress toppled over, unleashing the full fury of her majesty and her demon minions.

It was like someone yelled fire in a crowded theater. The group of once-enthralled bee lovers began fleeing for their lives, some jumping the neighbor's fence to the east, some jumping the neighbor's fence to the south, others heading northward to the street, all of them screaming and swatting wildly. The single bee buzzing around in my veil must've sensed the blow to her kingdom for she stuck her vicious stinger into my chin and held there pumping in her venom and swearing in bee-*ese*.

Suddenly suffused with an extra helping of adrenaline, I made my way through the stampeding crowd toward the house, pushing old ladies and elbowing children without regard.

As I retreated, I turned to look over my shoulder. Through the bobbing heads, flailing arms, and gyrating bodies of escapees, I saw a man in shorts rolling around on the ground yelling "Get away! Get away!", a screaming lady swinging her purse overhead like helicopter blades, and Bud, stripped down to nothing but his skivvies, hopping over the east neighbor's fence. Of course, there were also the scads of bees dive-bombing the retreating throngs. The whole thing was worse than the school children scene from Hitchcock's The Birds.

Passing the garage front, I noticed that the hot dogs had been left unattended and were ablaze, a four-foot-high tower of flames topped with a plume of gray smoke reaching skyward. Nothing I can do about it, I thought as I reached the kitchen side door and ducked into the house. Jenna and Sue were already in the kitchen, but I ran past them and their scowling faces toward the phone. Taped to the wall above the receiver was a list of emergency contacts, including the county bee inspector. Luckily, I had him on speed dial.

While the phone rang, I heard the ambulance go by and then Joseph called from the living room window.

"Mrs. Glaspy! The ambulance stopped at your house!" Sue ran out the front door hollering, "Buddy! My Buddy!"

"Hello?" a man on the phone answered.

"Inspector! Inspector!" I yelled into the receiver. "I tipped over my hive, and bees are everywhere! They attacked, a whole Mormon church and all of my neighbor's relatives!"

"Holy honey! Where are you at?"

"I'm in Ogden on Fifth Street, just follow the hot dog smoke and screaming hordes!" I hung up before the inspector could say anything else.

✳✳✳

After the bee inspector arrived and righted the hive, he let me know that it looked to be in good shape despite being dumped.

"Next time," he told me, "try smoking the bees before you open up the hive."

It had not occurred to me to try that, even though my beekeeper kit came with a smoker. I blame it on the video guy, who I suspect either staged his little show with some Hollywood trickery or put whiskey in his bees' sugar water before filming.

Over the next couple of hours, neighbors, church members, and Bud's relatives came over and picked up their food and hauled off the tables and chairs. To my surprise, none of the escapees were angry; not even the guy left rolling around on the ground. (To be fair though, I never did hear from the old ladies and kids who got in my way during the retreat.) Most of those who came back offered their condolences, and many of them still expressed interest in beekeeping. I couldn't believe it; after experiencing a natural and social disaster worthy of SWAT team crowd control and FEMA cleanup, all those people—neighbors, church members, even complete strangers—would still be supportive.

The day after the failed hive check, Bud returned home from the hospital. It turns out it wasn't the bee stings that put him in an ambulance. While he was hopping over the neighbor's fence, he broke the three smallest toes on his right foot. Since Sue wasn't home to drive him to the hospital, Bud called the ambulance. There wasn't much the doctors could do for his toes, but because he'd sustained thirty-seven bee stings, they advised him to stay the night.

"Bud, I'm *really* sorry about the failed hive check," I told him. "I know it's not what you probably had in mind—"

"Are you kiddin'?" Bud interrupted my apology. "That's the most fun and excitement I've had since moving into this neighborhood."

"What?"

"You bet! Who on earth would want a boring old normal hive check anyway? My only question is, when are we gonna do it again?"

"But, but," I stuttered, taken aback by Bud's response. "You...you ran away in your underwear and broke your toes in the process."

"Yeah, about running away in my underwear," Bud leaned over and pulled up his pant legs. "All but the sting on my arm and a couple on my back were on my legs." Several welts were still visible between Bud's knees and his socks. "Those bees found a hole in my snow pants and were making their way upward. I made a preemptive strike and ditched the clothes, fleeing for my house as fast as I could."

"And you want to do a hive check again?" I asked, laying on a thick incredulous tone.

"Absolutely! I'd love to see your hive succeed. Besides, what are the chances that a hive check could go that wrong again?"

"Well—"

"Plus, I'm hoping for a couple of jars of complimentary honey."

It would take me a couple of years to realize this, but Bud and a big chunk of the people in my community were truthfully interested in me and my well-being—they wanted me to succeed in self-reliance, at my career, with my family, in my spiritual endeavors, and yes, even with my beehive.

Indeed, I not only found a good house in which to make a good home, but I also found a good community in which I could feel truly at home.

UTAH or Bust!

Alice M Batzel

I once was a stranger to Brigham City and Box Elder County, and the tale of my journey here and my survival/adaptation after that is quite a tale to tell. I ask readers to keep in mind that my story exceeds the confines of this article, but the reading thereof will give you a glimpse of just who, how, and why one might choose Brigham City and Box Elder County as their destination and whether or not they choose to stay.

Nearly forty years ago I moved to Northern Utah from the Northwest Florida Gulf Coast. A question I've often heard since is, "Why in the world would you do that?" I'll admit, I was a beach girl and I would never consider taking my feet away from the Florida Ocean except for a mighty powerful reason—an employment opportunity for my husband. His job began on the Monday following his Friday interview. The abruptness of this change left one month of packing and moving to me, and five days of driving two thousand miles across the country with the assistance of only two little boys ages four and one-half years old and six years old. Often during that modern-day trek, I uttered, "Oh dear, this is going to be an adjustment." But it wasn't until after arriving in Brigham City that I realized the depth of the transformation that was before me.

As I drove into Brigham City, my boys and I saw beautiful mountains and the rural nature of the community on the East side of the interstate and the contrasting recreational water area of Willard Bay to the West. Seeing that there was a bit of a beach at the Willard Bay gave me a sense of relief that I had not entirely moved away from my beloved seaside. However, I was snapped into reality when my oldest son exclaimed, "Look Mom! Horses!" All I could say was, "Wow!" You see, he was looking at a group of about fifty cows. Yep, this was going to be an adjustment.

"Why are letters on the mountains? One says 'B,' and another one says 'I.' Where are the other letters?" I thought those were reasonable and logical questions that anyone might ask, even if they were from two little boys. "We'll have to ask your Dad," is all I could reply at that point; you see, I was still stunned about the horses that were cows. Seeing the alphabet on the mountains was something that puzzled even me.

We reunited with my husband at his place of employment, and then we went to the grocery store to get some supplies before going to our rental home. I asked the grocery cashier where I could find a copy of the daily newspaper. "Oh, it won't come out for five more days," she replied. Seeing that I was dazed and frozen by her comment, she explained that Brigham City had a weekly newspaper. My internal alarm was sounding, and I could hear the warning…yep, this is going to be an adjustment.

En route to our rental home, my husband drove out of Brigham City and explained that he had rented a home in nearby Bear River City. "Oh, you and the boys will love it. It's on a dairy farm, and there are cows all over the place, and the neighbors have a lot of kids. It'll be great fun for the boys." The boys were cheering, and I was cautiously optimistic. We drove past a huge cornfield, and as I looked out the window, I saw a wild animal jumping in the rows of corn. "I think I just saw a kangaroo," I told my husband. That immediately got the attention of the boys, and they strained their necks to see where I was pointing. "I don't know what you saw, but there are no kangaroos in Utah," my husband replied. "Well, it jumps like a kangaroo. What else could it be?" I asked. He had no solid answers. At this point, I was not too confident about living in a house on a remote dairy farm, with wild animals jumping like kangaroos in a cornfield, and my sons already thinking cows were horses. I was afraid to ask the obvious question about our community being called Bear River City.

We drove over a cement arch that crossed a large irrigation canal in front of our rental home then parked the station wagon on the driveway of the old farmhouse. A man exited out the side door and walked toward us. I could not mistake the fact that he was holding at least ten dead mice swinging by their tails from one of his hands. My husband made introductions to which the man simply nodded at me and told my husband that he had put one of his cats in our basement and that should get rid of "the problem." I wasn't so sure I wanted to enter our home. I didn't like cats, but more importantly, I didn't like mice. Though I had never seen one before, I was sure I didn't want to live with any. My little boys' eyes were as big as saucers, and they couldn't look away from the dead mice hanging from the man's hand. Yep, this was going to be an adjustment.

After unloading the station wagon of luggage and groceries, my husband announced that he had to go back into town for a rehearsal with his students in the school musical, and he would be back in a couple of hours. I put the boys to bed and sat down for a rest from that tiring day; shortly after that, was when I saw it—a mouse darted across the living room floor and crouched in the corner. I jumped on top of a dining room chair and grabbed a nearby umbrella as a potential defense weapon. I sat perched on the chair, and the mouse stayed in his corner until my husband returned two hours later. After he killed the mouse by smashing it with a laundry hamper, my husband surrendered my broken umbrella as a casualty from his first attempt. My first night in Utah, and we had killed a wild animal in our home. Yep, this was going to be an adjustment.

Our boys were sound asleep, and as soon as I drifted to sleep, I abruptly sat up when I heard loud animal noises outside our bedroom window. "I think there's a moose at our window," I whispered to my husband who seemed to sleep through the disturbance. I looked out the curtain and was faced with a large cow staring back at me. I gasped, but I didn't scream or faint—I was proud of that fact. My husband stirred a bit and said, "It's just a cow. Come back to bed." It was obvious that he had no concerns about living in the wilderness. But I wasn't confident the adjustment was going to be as easy or as sure as he implied it would be. I had only been here one day, my boys thought cows were horses, the mountains had letters of the alphabet on them, there was only a weekly newspaper, kangaroos were in the cornfield, mice and a cat were in our basement, we killed a mouse in the living room, and stray dairy cows were at my bedroom window. I could wait no longer. I had to ask. "Are there any bears out here in Bear River City?"

It's been nearly 40 years since my arrival in Brigham City, and I can honestly say that my husband and I love living here. We've worked long careers in education and healthcare, raised our family, and have very fond admiration for our first Utah friends in Bear River City. I look forward to the weekly newspaper, smile every time I see the B or the I on the nearby mountains as I recall learning their meaning. We've witnessed weddings, births of babies, and funerals of dear friends. We've seen community growth, witnessed a few squabbles over water and irrigation issues, campaigned for elected officials, volunteered, attended county fairs and rodeos, and participated in Peach Days and Promontory's Golden Spike Reenactment. I've discovered that deer sometimes jump like a kangaroo. I've learned how to quilt, bottle fruit, make bread, and do a bit of domestic gardening. We've worshiped here, laughed, and shed tears. Our home is here. I still miss the ocean, but whenever I take a trip to visit our relatives along the Northwest Florida seashore, I have never felt so "at home" as when I come back to Brigham City, the mountains that surround it, and our Box Elder County.

The Bear Lake Monster

Tyler Brian Nelson

You know there are some things in this world that you've got to see to believe. Then even when you see them, you don't believe your eyes. But I know what I saw, so I'll tell you about it. My name is Nathaniel, and oh boy, do I have a story for you. I don't believe that there had ever been a drearier day around the states when I reached the top of that hill and looked down on the grand lake stretching out before me.

The skies were clouding over something fierce, and the water was churning up, ready for a storm. My old trousers were tattered to pieces, my shirt was falling to rags, and I'd nearly worn my shoes through. But that steely cold wind did my soul some good. I didn't know the name of the lake then, but I knew that I was close enough to Utah to be in the clear. I'd had a bad game of cards back in Boise, got up a few dollars and those old gamblers thought I was cheating. A few hot words led to punches, and that led to the boys at the bar and the proprietor asking a price on my head, so I decided it was time to skip town. Those hard winters were for the dogs anyway, and I was longing for somewhere sunny. So, I packed my bags and set off down the road real quick. Those darned sheriffs seemed to have it out for me though. They had dogged me for the past month, and I had to hop from town to town like a scared jackrabbit. But now I'd made it; those Idaho boys couldn't touch me.

It was getting to be real late evening by the time I found a town to wander into, and that peculiar storm that had hung over my head all day finally went and did what it had been threatening to do, and the heavens came down with a vengeance. I dashed down the muddy street until I spotted an old hotel. I hopped on the porch and watched the rain batter the little town for a moment then slipped through the doors. I pushed through the entry hall toward the sound of voices buzzing at the end of the far hall. I found myself in a bar. The warm room was filled to the rafters with grizzled fur trappers and crusty fishermen, all of them laughing and sloshing their mugs about.

"Ho, a newcomer!" shouted a mountain of a man in the middle of the room as he spotted me.

"And he's wet as a fish!" cried an old codger near the fire. "Jeb, did you drag him in on your hook?" The whole room roared with laughter.

"Don't you mind them, boy," the barman called from the counter, "just come on in and dry up by the fire there. One of you mongrels give him a drink!"

"Thank you kindly," I said as the codger shifted across the bench to make room by the fire. The old man shook his head.

"What the devil were you doing out with a storm like that coming in? Heaven knows your taking your chances walking about in weather like this!"

I smirked and then chuckled. "I've been making way my down from Idaho; I'm heading south for warmer weather."

The mountain man rumbled his way over and pushed another man off the end of the bench. He sat down and flashed a smile at me.

"Warmer weather or a cooler attitude you're heading for?"

"Well I, I'm just uh..." I stammered out.

The man threw back his huge head and shook the rafters with his booming laugh.

"No problem here, boy, you ain't the first one to come through our town on the lam. In fact, half of 'em are still here, ain't that right, Jocko?" He jumped up to slap the back of a slick-looking fellow in a long coat. The man winced and scurried away, checking back over his shoulder.

The barman brought over a set of fresh drinks and handed them out.

"Yes," he said, "we sure get one or two with some color coming through now and again, but we don't take any names and try to keep our business ours, and their business theirs. Some give us trouble, but they don't last long. Just last month—"

A clap of thunder came crashing from the sky at the same moment the back doors of the bar crashed open, and a menacing silhouette stepped over the threshold. Every man in the room jumped and held their breath, eyeing the specter with fear. As the man stepped into the room, the trappers and fishers relaxed and began to chuckle.

"Why it's just old Ceran!" laughed the mountain man, "any luck on the catch today?" The men laughed. Ceran stuck his chest out and eyed the huge man.

"Well enough, and I'll thank you to keep your nose out of my business!"

The man shook his head. "You don't have any business, you old fool, and if you knew what was good for you, you'd stay off the lake in these hurricanes!"

Ceran muttered something into his beard and made his way to a stool and sat down heavily.

"What's with him?" I asked.

"He's just a loon who likes to fish in the rain," the old man said.

"Well, I've never seen a more sodden down fisher than that. He looks like he might fall to pieces any minute."

"Well, he just might," said the big man, "you see his foot?"

"Wooden?"

"Aye and try to shake his hand if you're up to it, you'll not find much there for shaking."

I craned my neck to get a better look at the old fisher. "What happened to him?"

The old man bent forward and lowered his voice. "He won't say much often, but when he does, you'll get him going on and on about a monster."

"A monster?"

"Yes, these Indians around here have a legend about it. Some kind of creature in the water. Comes out to snatch up cattle and kids alike. Most of the locals don't like to talk about it, including Tommy the barman there. Speaking of the devil, here he comes. Not a word more boy."

Tommy came back, and the conversation drifted away, but I kept an eye on Ceran.

After a few hours the rain let up a bit, and the men began to drift out the doors. As Ceran got off his stool and tottered to the doors, I jumped after him. Ceran looked me up and down wearily as I approached. I stuck out my hand to shake.

"My name is Nathaniel; you must be Ceran."

The gnarled fisherman eyed my hand for a moment and then stuck out his own. The pointer and the middle finger were missing, cut clean off from the first knuckle of both.

"Ceran. The town crazy as I am sure you've been told."

"Well people talk, but I don't always put my whole stock into what everybody says. You're a fisherman then?" I asked.

"As much as I can be anymore, with this wooden walker and not much of a hand left, it's tough to get by."

I shook my head in sympathy.

"Understandable, it's quite the injury. I don't mean to pry, but can I ask how it happened?"

Ceran stared at me for a while. "You might. Do you fish?"

"I do. I worked on a sailing ship off the coast of California for a while, and we held our own."

Ceran stared at me again for a moment.

"Would you be willing to help out with a bit of fishing? I could use a spot of assistance, and I could tell you the story while we set about it."

"I don't see why not," I said.

"Good, then meet me at the north marina at sundown tomorrow. I'll have the gear."

"A deal it is," I agreed. We shook hands again, and Ceran shuffled out into the night.

The next day the skies cleared up a bit, so I took in the sights of the lake and the town. Turns out I had stumbled into a little trading town just south of the border called Garden City. Though how much it looked like a garden, I didn't know. The town was set on the west edge of a great clear blue lake, which the locals call Black Bear Lake, or sometimes just Bear Lake. The locals seemed to have a good taste for the raspberries that grew in abundance around the valley, and the trappers were happy to snap them up too. As the sun started to go down, I set off for the docks.

When I reached the dock, Ceran was waiting for me.

"Everything's in order; we can launch out straight away. Where's your boat?"

"That's her right there."

"That tiny thing?"

It was tiny, indeed, a little old rowboat. Two oars lay at the ready, and a spear and a pair of ropes lay on the bottom.

"Well, where are your line and bait?" I asked.

"I've got all we need, and here's the bait."

He picked up a brown sack and threw it to me. I caught it tentatively and nearly lost my dinner when the smell hit me. I held it away from me and asked:

"Ceran, what is this?"

"It's just the trick," he said with a twinkle in his eye.

I was rapidly losing faith in the fishing part of the trip, but I was interested in the story, so I went with it. We set off in the boat, me rowing and Ceran fidgeting with his rope. I rowed until we were square in the middle of the lake and then Ceran called for a stop.

"Let me set this good, and then I'll tell you my story," he said.

He bent down for the brown bag and pulled out a rancid chunk of meat the size of my head. The smell nearly pushed me overboard, but Ceran calmly took his first rope and tied it around the meat. When he had got it good and tight, he threw it out over the water. The disgusting bait splashed down into the clear water and then bobbed to the surface.

Ceran watched it for a moment and then sat back down in the boat. I watched the whole thing in wonder, Ceran's strange methods baffling me.

"Now we wait a minute," he said, "and I'll tell you my story."

We sat in the silence of the night and watched the moon come up and glisten off the water. Storm clouds to the south rose over the mountains and began a steady march in our direction. After a good long while, Ceran shifted in his seat.

"Well, I guess it's time I told you my story." He closed his eyes and took a deep breath. "It was a night much like this one. I was a younger man, just come up over from the east. I'd heard about good trapping and trail living, so I thought I might try my hand. On one of the slower days of trading there in town, I decided I'd go out fishing for an evening. I got a boat a bit bigger than this one, and a line and I rowed on out. I didn't catch a single fish. Not even a bite so I decided I would head back in.

As I was rowing, I spotted something a few yards off. It looked like a boat that had gone belly up, and I was concerned someone had fallen into some trouble. But as I started rowing towards it, the thing slid under the water, and I saw that it wasn't any boat. Boats aren't a sickly green, and they sure don't have scales. I took to rowing as fast as I could the other way, but I was too late. Looking over my shoulder, I saw the monster! Big as life and with enough teeth to make me scream. I rowed for my life! But the monster was so fast. He made to swallow me and my boat in one go, but I jumped clear with not a second to spare.

The boat went to pieces, and I was all full of water and couldn't see a thing. Then it got me by the foot. Nothing ever hurt so much in my life! The beast grabbed me and dragged me down, heading for the bottom. I couldn't get my wits about me, couldn't breathe, so I started lashing out. I found the mouth of the thing and where it had me by the foot and started pulling real hard. But the thing bit down again, and I lost all my senses."

"My goodness, man! How did you survive that?" I asked. Ceran shook his head.

"Some other fellows heard a commotion off in the darkness and came to investigate. When they arrived, all they found was me, half-drowned and missing a few pieces. They rowed me back to shore as fast as they could, and lucky for me I pulled through it after a couple of weeks. But I never forgot the hungry look in that beast's eye. To this day, it makes my blood boil! The monster took my foot, and my fingers, and my life!"

"Come on, Ceran, it's not all that bad," I said. "You still manage to get around and do your fishing all right."

Ceran barked out a shaky laugh. He looked at me directly in the eyes, his eyes wide, and his smile crooked.

"Those crooks in town just think I'm an old crow who likes to fish in the rain. I'm not out here for the fish boy; I'm out here for revenge!"

My jaw very nearly hit the bottom of the boat. I'd been so stupid, how had I missed it? The strange meat, the ropes, the spear. Ceran wasn't looking for cisco or whitefish; he was hunting for a lake monster! I jumped to my feet, nearly tipping the boat.

"You dragged me out here in the night to hunt for some sea monster! Ceran, we are two men in a tiny boat! What were you going to do if you found it again?"

Ceran shot to his feet, almost dumping us in the water. "I'm going to send the creature to a watery grave where it belongs!"

I shook my head and took a step back in the boat.

"You're off your rocker, and this fishing trip is over!"

I turned and sat down on my seat. "Hand me those oars; I'm going to row us back in. Ceran? Hand me the oar! Ceran?"

I looked back. Ceran was staring at the water and standing frozen still. A smile slowly crept onto his face. His eyes flicked to me, and I was scared to see a sharp glint of glee in them.

"This trip is far from over boy."

He looked back out over the water. I followed his gaze to try and see what he was looking at. Nothing, just waves—growing higher. Nothing. No bobbing, rancid meat. I felt the blood drain from my face.

"Ceran, where did the bait go?" I stammered. He just laughed and snatched up his spear.

"Here she comes." He whispered. "Here she comes."

A few yards out into the water, I could see the ripples of huge bubbles break on the waves. I watched in horror as a huge head rose out of the water. Big, green, and scaly it had enough teeth to make one of them great ocean sharks turn tail. The great beast hissed as it rose. Its eyes met mine, and my heart nearly stopped. They were cold and hungry, hungry for me, I knew it.

I let out a scream of fear just as Ceran let out a bellow of anger and threw his spear. It hit the monster square in the eye, and the creature made a sound I hope never to hear again. Like a great metal riverboat grinding on the rocks of the shore, the monster screeched in pain.

"I got it! I got it!" Ceran yelled.

"Ceran! We've got to go! We've got to—" But he wasn't listening. He was howling with glee while the monster writhed in pain. Suddenly it reared up its great head and looked at us with its good eye. It glared down on us for a moment, its eye full of anger.

"Ceran!"

Then it lunged at us. With just a second to spare, I pushed Ceran out of the boat and leaped clear. The monster smashed the boat to pieces. I swallowed a mouthful of water and came up coughing. Waves were crashing, and the monster was writhing madly. I couldn't see Ceran through the tempest. The monster lashed out again, and I dove back under the water. I felt a sharp pain in the back of my head, and everything went black.

I woke up two days later at the hotel in Garden City. Some fishermen had found me floating in boat debris, half-drowned and with a lump on my head. They had heard a commotion from shore and came out to investigate. But they found no Ceran and no monster. I know it's there, though. It has been a long time since I found my warm southern weather, but I know that up in that beautiful blue lake on the Utah-Idaho border, something is swimming in the deep. So be careful what you go fishing for. You just might find it.

Fishing with Heber Stock

Kathy Davidson

Bear Lake lies across the border between Utah and Idaho. It has the most beautiful blue waters seen this side of the Caribbean. Most people know it as a paradise of the Rockies. I grew up in a village on Bear Lake's shore.

The lake serves all kinds of people. The farmers downstream use it to store water for their crops. The depths are great for training scuba divers. The swimmers and water skiers love the shallow beaches. Then there are the fishermen. This is my group. There are four breeds of fish that are found no other place on earth; Bonneville Cisco, Bear Lake Whitefish, Bear Lake Sculpin, and the Bonneville Whitefish. The Cisco is a small greasy fish mostly used for bait.

What I remember best about growing up near Bear Lake is Heber Stock, our next-door neighbor. Heber was old when I was three. He was withered and bowlegged. His back was so bent he couldn't stand up straight, and still, he was taller than my dad. He was so old he lived before there were cars and rode horses everywhere. He built a house for his bride by cutting trees on the mountains and dragging them back to town behind a horse. He was a cowboy, and he was my hero. I wanted to be like him when I grew up. He had adventures most people only read about. I loved to sit and listen to the stories about his life. It was better than reading Zane Gray.

When I knew him, Heber spent most of his time gardening or fishing. He would go every day, rain or shine, winter or summer. He loved living by the lake and knew everything about it.

He told me it was the minerals in the water that reflected the color of the sky. In the morning the lake reflects a silver color that bounces the sun back-- it appears to glow. In the afternoon the lake is the most perfect turquoise blue. Heber taught me the deepest part of the lake, near two hundred feet deep, reflected the darkest blues. The shallow shores don't reflect the blue as well and look glassy. Heber taught me about the wind picking up in the afternoons and making the lake downright dangerous. That's one of the reasons Heber only fished in the mornings and spent his afternoons in the garden. Otherwise, he would be out on the lake all day.

In the early afternoons, when my chores were done, or whenever I could escape the work, I loved to climb through the fence and visit with Heber while he worked in his garden. Heber showed me mole holes under his carrots and the eggs in the bird's nest in his apple trees. He also told me about his fishing trips. They seemed magical — more than anything, I wanted to go fishing on Bear Lake with him.

The morning my father announced we were going ice fishing with Heber was the best day of my life. I packed up my warm clothes and got ready for amazing adventures we were about to have.

Heber once told me about the time he and his buddy Don went ice fishing. Don had worked in the mines and was on oxygen. He wheezed as he breathed, sounding like Darth Vader. His ever-present oxygen tank didn't seem to bother Heber. They had been friends since the old days. Heber would pack Don, the portable oxygen tank, food, and the fishing gear into a sled he could pull behind his snowmobile, and they would be off for a day on the lake. The ice was only thick in spots that year, so they went on the south end, near Laketown where the ice was thicker. After a fun-filled day of fishing, they packed everything on top of Don in the sled, Heber started up the machine, and they headed home. They hadn't gone far when they found the ice had floated, creating a twenty-foot gap of open water. By the time Heber noticed the gap, it was too late to turn around. He did the only thing he knew; he gunned it. The snowmobile skidded across the water, dragging Don in the sled behind to the ice on the other side of the gap.

I asked him if he was afraid Don might have drowned. He said, "Na, he had his oxygen."

I laughed and couldn't wait to experience the adventure for myself.

We loaded all our gear onto the ice, drilled a hole and then I waited. When was the adventure going to start? I watched the ice close to see if it would float us away. I nearly jumped out of my skin when the ice moaned. I whooped when a thundering crack sliced by. Heber didn't even look up. I understand now my father would never agree to go fishing if the ice wasn't two feet deep over the entire lake. We did a lot of sitting-- a lot of it. We only caught three fish, and one of them was less than the legal length to keep. It was nothing to brag about. I was so disappointed I didn't beg to go ice fishing again. I thought maybe summer fishing would be more of an adventure.

Heber had so many stories about fishing in a boat. He once told me about a time he took the Utah Fish and Game wardens fishing. They needed help checking the fish population. Heber met them on Cisco Beach on the east side of the lake, Utah side. They went out in the state boat. It's a nice one, big enough to rescue tourists in the rough waters. Heber agreed to go just so he could enjoy the luxury boat. He told them to go above Rock Pile. The bottom of the lake at this spot is covered with porous rock instead of sand. The little fish like to hide there, so a plethora of bigger fish hunt there. This was where Heber snagged a little rock that looks like a rocking sea horse.

He had to stop his story and show the rock to me. He kept it on the windowsill by his back door. If I used my imagination a little, I could see the sea horse, and the base isn't flat, so it does rock. I was impressed.

Well, Heber was fishing with the wardens, and he got a bite. It was a big one. One of the wardens grabbed the net and helped get the fish into the boat. Heber watched as they examined the fish, measured the length and weight, pinned a tag on, and threw it back.

Heber looked at me with his shocked face. His big old face looked bigger, and his mouth hung open. "Can you believe those daggum wardens threw my fish back!" His eyes wide, he looked at me until I was indignant enough for him. "I had to watch one of the biggest fish I've ever caught swim away. I almost jumped in to go after it."

I had seen many of his large fish. He even had one mounted on his wall. So, I imagined it was maybe even bigger than me.

Well, he said he mumbled a few choice words under his breath. He didn't tell me the words, just let me use my imagination. The wardens chuckled and went back to their own lines. Heber said he grumped for a while until the wardens got him a soda and all was forgiven--until the next fish was caught. Heber was shocked to see the same thing happen again. The warden grabbed the net, the fish, weight, length, tag, and back into the water. This time Heber said he didn't just mumble those words. He turned his back on the wardens and wouldn't talk to them. They tried to laugh it off, but Heber wasn't having it. The next fish Heber caught on his line; he was going to take home to his wife. The wardens agreed to let him. It wasn't as big as the first fish he caught, in fact, it was barely big enough to keep legally, but the wardens agreed Heber had earned it and let him keep his catch.

I wanted to fish and catch three fish I could keep. I wanted to be able to tell my friends about the big fish Heber would help me catch. The day finally came the next summer. My dad and I went fishing with Heber. It was another boring day. I didn't catch anything. I watched Heber catch a fish. He didn't even use a pole. Instead, he slipped a line over his finger and bobbed it up and down in the water. I tried it myself, but the line cut my finger. It burned like a paper cut. I sucked on it for a minute as Heber showed the calluses he had developed on his finger from years of fishing without a pole.

Heber took us to the east side of the lake and showed us the bank where the mountain drops steeply into the water. The park service had sunk some cars to keep the bank from eroding. The scuba divers like to use this beach for training. Because of the lake's high elevation, a scuba diver can certify for deep water, without going deep. It brings good business to the people around the lake.

Heber told us another story as we sat bobbing our poles in the water. He was fishing with Don and another friend Evan. Evan is the young one of the famous trio. He retired early because of his bad heart.

He and the boys (he called them boys, but they were older than my grandpa) put out their lines and sat watching the divers come in and out of the water. The fish weren't biting, and the boys were getting too much sun, so Heber decided to give up for the day. They left their lines in as they motored to shore. Evan, with his bad heart, was elected to watch the lines as Don helped Heber load the gear and the boat in the back of the truck. When they had just about finished loading, Evan yelled out, "Heber's line has a tug." Heber rushed over and started fighting the fish. It was a strong fighter, and he figured he caught a real big one this time. The two struggled, in and out, the fish winning, then Heber winning, then the fish took out more line. Heber worked the line carefully so it wouldn't break. He doesn't want to lose the fish or his favorite lure. They continued to fight, in and out. After about thirty minutes, the line went still. Heber tugs. It won't give. It's stuck somewhere. The fish wasn't pulling out either. Somewhere between the fish and Heber, the line was caught. Don suggested maybe one of the divers might go down and unsnag the line and perhaps bring the fish back with him. Evan volunteered to ask and soon finds a willing diver to go see what was going on down there. The three friends wait for what seemed like an hour but was probably only fifteen minutes before the diver came back to the surface.

"There's a car down there, and the fish is inside," he tells Heber. "The window isn't open enough for me to reach in."

Heber and the boys are at a loss. They don't want to go home empty-handed or without Heber's favorite lure. So, they get this idea to send down a gaff hook with the diver to stab the fish and bring it back. One of the other divers has one and sends it back down to get the fish. The diver was gone even longer this time. Heber felt his line loosen and figures it's been cut. They get excited to see the big fish. But the diver comes up empty-handed.

"What happened? Where's my fish?" Heber demanded of the diver.

"Sorry, I tried. Every time I reached in to get the fish; he rolled the window up further."

Dad chuckled, and I realize the fish really didn't do that. I was disappointed again, and my dad tells me it's just a story, and most all fishing trips are just about sitting and enjoying the quiet lake and thinking up stories to tell. He said I must not be old enough to appreciate it yet.

Well, I got old enough to appreciate it. I don't get the luxury to enjoy fishing on the calm waters of Bear Lake as often as I would like. But I do think up stories to tell. They aren't as wild as Heber's or always about fishing. I love telling them, though. Making my face all long with my mouth hanging open or motioning the way he did when he caught the big one. I guess in a way, I grew up to be like Heber Stock after all. My life is as exciting as a Zane Gray novel -- in my imaginations.

The Road from Grief

J Audrey Hammer

Brian exited the Provo Municipal Airport with a carry-on bag over his shoulder and his father's ashes in a box under his arm. He looked around warily at the taxis and shuttles waiting for passengers, unsure which to take. He was supposed to go to Saint George but had ended up here thanks to wildfires in the southwest part of the state. Before he had a chance to look more closely, one of the shuttle drivers approached him.

"Hey! I'm Rodney!" Rodney's clothes and hands were grimy, and he hadn't shaved in days. Or maybe that was just the style he kept his beard. "You heading south?"

"Yes, actually, I need to get to—"

"Great! I've got space, and my rates are great. I'll even give you half off since I bet you didn't mean to end up in Provo, did you?"

"Uh—" Brian looked around at the other taxis, quickly filling up with passengers. At least Rodney appeared sober. That was what really mattered, right? "Can you get me to Canyonlands?"

"Absolutely!" Rodney enthused.

"Well, why not. Lead the way, Rodney."

Rodney's shuttle was a nine-passenger van. It was spacious and comfy enough. There was already one passenger aboard in the passenger seat. She looked to be about twenty years old. She had brown hair streaked with blonde coloring and was chewing gum. She was also smiling broadly.

"I'm Hannah," she said as Brian slid into the seat behind the driver. "I flew into Salt Lake, so it's just been Rodney and me for the last hour."

Well, she didn't seem any worse for wear. "Hi, I'm Brian."

Rodney settled in and started up the van. "A couple more quick stops, and we'll hit the road."

He pulled up near the student center at BYU. Two students got in, a boy and a girl. The boy headed for the very back while the girl sat across from Brian.

As the van pulled away, Hannah turned around in her seat to greet them. "Brynlee? Is that you?"

The girl addressed as Brynlee looked up at Hannah. "Hannah?! Oh my gosh!"

Then both girls were screaming and trying to hug each other.

"I guess you know each other," Brian observed, discreetly putting his hands over his ears.

"We're cousins!" the girls shouted, more or less together.

Hannah explained, "We're going to a family reunion in Moab. My dad is the second oldest in his family, and Hannah's mom is his sister, who's the fourth one in the family. There were six kids. But we're also going to see second cousins there and great-aunts and great-uncles."

Hannah then launched into a history of her family's genealogy and how they were all connected, exactly. Brian soon zoned out and looked at the box on his lap. It was made of stained wood and was rectangular with a delicate filigree carved around the edges. His dad had made it a long time ago. He'd liked doing things with his hands, liked being outdoors, and liked meeting people from all over the place. He'd believed everyone had an interesting story about them. Now he was gone. Had Brian said everything he'd meant to? Had he had all the conversations he'd wanted? He didn't know. But they were done whether he liked it or not.

Brian watched the traffic out the window. An odd pattern was happening. There it was again … and again.

"Nobody on the road is driving in their own lane!" he blurted out, watching cars drifting toward each other.

"There's only two that are barely drifting," Rodney defended. "You can't expect every single one to drive straight."

Brian was pretty sure he could expect such a thing.

They drove for a while longer, the two cousins speaking rapidly and not noticing anyone else yet. Rodney turned up the traffic report on the radio.

"… where the north lane on eastbound 215 is blocked near 6500 South …"

Brian tried to wrap his head around it. Had the announcer managed to insert every point of the compass in a traffic report? What was first? North lane … what the heck did that mean?

"No problem there," Rodney said and switched through the stations as he tried to find a traffic report for farther south.

As Rodney got ready to exit the interstate, a car from the far-left lane drove nearly horizontally across them to catch the exit. Rodney had to brake hard to avoid a collision.

They headed into the canyon, following a twisty, windy road that soon had Brian holding his breath and gripping his seat as discreetly as he could. He wished Rodney would drive a little slower. A lot little slower. The cousins continued talking softly. The student in the back just watched out the window.

"Isn't this beautiful country?" Rodney asked conversationally.

"Oh, yeah," Brian said to be agreeable. He just wished he didn't have to enjoy it from the edge of a cliff.

"This road can be dangerous, but I've driven it hundreds of times. Relax and enjoy the view."

Brian tried. And it really was a great view with vibrant fall colors scattered along the mountain.

"So you're heading to Canyonlands, right, Brian?" Rodney asked.

"That's right."

The cousins stopped talking to take an interest. Hannah asked, "Are you meeting someone there?"

"I'm spreading my father's ashes there."

That made everyone quiet for a moment.

Brynlee said, "I'm so sorry for your loss. I'm all excited for a family reunion, and that must be torturing you! I'm so thoughtless."

Truthfully, Brian hadn't been paying that close attention to the girls, but he said, "No, you're fine. Thank you. My father loved the outdoors and went camping everywhere. It fell to me to take him out one last time. Where is your reunion?"

"Moab. We'll be doing a lot of outdoor stuff there."

"Sounds great," Brian said.

"How about you in the back there?" Rodney called. "What's your name again?"

The student was startled. "Hunter."

"And where are you getting off?"

"Monticello."

"That's pretty isolated. What's there for you?"

"Just going to my aunt and uncle's for the summer. Going to help on the ranch and stuff. It's pretty boring."

But Brynlee wasn't having any of it. She quizzed him all about ranching and his time at school. Brian was impressed at how she got him to talk about himself without inserting herself into the conversation at all. Perhaps he had misjudged her as being flighty and self-absorbed.

Brian looked out the windshield again. "That car has had its left blinker for the last ten miles," he remarked. "Where's he going? Off the cliff?"

"Like your California drivers are so great?" Hannah retorted.

Brian shrugged. She had a point.

When they finally reached the town of Price after the harrowing ride through the canyon, the car turned right at the first intersection. Brian figured that would at least automatically turn the blinker off.

Rodney stopped the van at a local burger joint so they could eat and left them while he picked up another passenger.

"I used to come here all the time on road trips," Hunter said.

The three young people all ordered root beer and extra fry sauce. Brian stuck to Coke and was afraid to ask what fry sauce was until they pushed it on him like manic drug dealers.

"It's good, right? Try it! Try it!"

Brian humored them and decided it was a worthy condiment, if not deserving of such enthusiastic worship. The meal helped calm his nerves after the recent drive. Rodney pulled into the parking lot as they were finishing up.

The new passenger was an elderly woman now sitting in the passenger seat, which Hannah had given up for her.

"Hey, kids," Rodney greeted as they filed into the van. "This is Myrtle Cogswell. She's a regular."

"Hello, Sister Cogswell!" Hannah said cheerfully, greeting her with a half handshake, half hug.

They must know each other, too, Brian thought after the rather intimate greeting.

"It's nice to meet you!" Hannah continued.

Maybe not. How does Hannah know she's Mormon? Did she just assume it? "Sister" Cogswell didn't object to the title in any case.

The cousins sat in the back row. Brian took his original seat, and Hunter moved to the middle.

They had just gotten on the road again when there was a jolt; it was a flat tire.

"Ah, dagnabit," Rodney cursed.

"Oh, my heck!" Brynlee exclaimed.

Brian stifled a laugh.

Rodney inched over to the side of the road and got out to examine the tire. Hunter immediately jumped out to help. The three women all looked at Brian expectantly, so he got out, too.

"There's a tire place just down the road," Rodney said. "I'm not sure if it's worth putting the spare on. I think I'll just walk down and get one."

Two young men in suits on bicycles pulled up by them. "Hey, can we give you a hand?" They had name badges identifying them as Elder Jennings and Elder Hickman. Brian thought they were awfully young to be "elders."

Rodney shrugged. "I'm just heading out to buy a tire if you feel like joining me."

Elder Jennings got off his bike. "Here. Why don't you take my bike? It'll be faster. They'll drive you back here; I'll pick up my bike when we're done. We'll wait here for you."

Rodney shrugged again and got on the bike. Brian couldn't believe someone just gave a stranger his bicycle. The possibility that he might not get it back didn't even seem to occur to the young man.

"Are you all on vacation?" the other elder asked.

"Sort of," Hunter said. "Just finished the semester. Where you from?"

"Southern Indiana."

"No way!" Hunter exclaimed. "I'm from Chandler."

"You gotta be kidding! Do you know President Lewis, then?"

"That's my dad."

"Oh my gosh. That's crazy."

"What's your name?" Hunter squinted at the name badge.

"Elder Hickman. Sam."

The two of them continued to discover mutual friends and acquaintances and stories they'd heard about these people. Brian just stood in wonder at the coincidence of it all.

Eventually, Rodney turned up in a truck with the bike in the back. The two missionaries insisted on helping change the tire, which was probably more help than Rodney needed or wanted.

Brian said to Hunter, "I guess our job here is done."

Back in the car, Mrs.—Sister—Cogswell asked Brian where he was headed.

"Canyonlands."

"Oh, that's a lovely area," she replied. "So many visitors end up missing it. Have you been before?"

"Yes, with my dad. It was his favorite place. That's why I'm taking his ashes there." He held up the box.

Mrs. Cogswell raised an eyebrow but didn't comment.

"Aren't you supposed to have an urn, not a box?" Hunter asked.

"Dad made it himself. He said if he was going to be scattered to the four winds, he didn't need some ugly urn for the job."

Sister Cogswell asked, "Did you already have the funeral?"

"Yes. My family is pretty spread out, so it was nice seeing everyone."

"Has your ward brought you meals?"

"My what?"

"Brian's not a Mormon, Myrtle," Rodney explained.

"Oh. Well, where do you live right now?"

"Mendocino, California."

"Write down your address for me, and I'll make sure you're taken care of."

The thought of food must have taken hold in the cousins' minds, as they began talking about a showcase of family recipes at the reunion while Brian wrote down his address.

"Aunt Martha is bringing her strawberry-rhubarb pie," Hannah said. "And Grandma has her Jell-O salad."

"Excellent. Mom is bringing her famous funeral potatoes," Brynlee said.

"Uncle Dan is doing food-storage wheat bread."

"Hmm," Brynlee answered without enthusiasm.

Brian's brain had just gone from wondering how Jell-O could be called a salad to wondering what funeral potatoes were, and why such an ominous-sounding dish was going to be featured at a family reunion sure to be crowded with the elderly.

"Wait," he interrupted, "funeral potatoes? What's that?"

"Potatoes that are served at funerals," Hannah explained. "Though you can have them anytime."

"I'm going to have them at my wedding!" Brynlee said excitedly.

"Oh, are you engaged? When's the big day?" Brian asked.

"Oh, no, I don't have a fiancé or a boyfriend," Brynlee replied. "I'm just planning ahead."

"So how are they different from other potatoes, taste-wise?"

"It's basically a potato casserole, sort of a mix of hash browns, soup, and cheese."

"Huh. Isn't that pretty much au gratin potatoes?"

"What's that?"

Mrs. Cogswell left the shuttle first, in Green River. Hannah and Brynlee were the next to leave as the shuttle arrived in Moab. Rodney decided it would be easier to drop off Brian before Hunter.

"Just us men now," Rodney said.

It was a quiet, peaceful drive. By the time Brian stepped out of the car at long last, he was already in a contemplative mood. With the warm desert air drifting across his face and gravel crunching under his shoes, it was like being in another world. It was still and quiet and vast and empty. He spent the next few days with his thoughts and his dad, marveling at the strange, unique beauty of the desert rocks. He was going to be okay. He was still going to miss his dad terribly, but it would be okay.

✳✳✳

Back home, he was getting used to his routine again when his doorbell rang one evening. There was a woman there holding what appeared to be a nacho casserole.

"Hello, Brian? I'm Sister Ramirez. I understand you've had a death in the family? I'm so sorry. We'll be bringing you food for a few days to give you one less thing to worry about."

"That's really not nec—" Brian gave up.

"Sister Cogswell in Utah was very concerned about you."

Brian couldn't help but feel touched. "I don't suppose you have funeral potatoes?"

"Sorry, what?"

"Never mind. It's a Utah thing."

Rats

Mike Nelson

It was a hot July day on the dairy farm in Willard when Gary and Walter went to the old granary to pick up some calf feed. The farm hadn't used the granary to store loose grain for several years, but the round, galvanized-steel building appeared to be the perfect place to store the paper sacks of feed to keep them out of the weather.

The so-called grain bin didn't have an ordinary door, and whereas it wasn't easy to build a square door to fit a round building, one of the farmhands had simply cut a rough opening in the side of the metal building to allow easy access. Without a door to cover the opening, there was no way to keep critters out; but until that day, nobody had seemed to care.

To keep the feed sacks up off the granary floor, where they'd be ruined by moisture, the farmhands had laid old wooden pallets end-to-end, and side-by-side across the entire floor.

To keep the feed sacks from sagging through the space between the slats or getting torn open by the loose nails in the slats, they had laid a carpet of burlap sacks across the pallets to form a soft floor of sorts to lay the sacks on.

This particularly hot day, the first thing they both noticed when they walked inside the grain bin was the stench. Rodents in general leave behind a rather pungent odor, and from the smell wafting up around them, they assumed that several mice had found the calf feed (Rats were the furthest thing from their minds at that point).

As they began to move the paper sacks, feed drained out of holes that had been chewed in the bags, and it soon became obvious from the number of damaged bags, that they had a significant rodent problem.

They decided to remove all of the feed, and then deal with what they found once the building was empty.

A while later, all that remained visible above the wooden pallet floor was a layer of burlap, punctuated by small mounds of spilled feed. Incredibly they hadn't seen a single mouse. When Gary pulled back the layer of burlap that covered the first pallet, he saw a dark fuzzy substance filling nearly every opening between the slats. As he shifted position to get a better view, that substance moved! What he was seeing was the hairy backs of scores of enormous rats!

Now a normal, thinking person, would have immediately retreated in horror and sought a sane remedy for the destruction of what appeared to be a mind-bending sea of rodents.

The testosterone-fueled male brain; however, is not often known for reasonable thought, and in this case, Gary and Walter saw the opportunity for what appeared to be a great deal of adrenaline-filled fun, i.e., rat bashing.

Did I mention that Walter was in his sixties and Gary was roughly half his age? In the end, it's amazing that Walter didn't have a heart attack over what happened next.

I think Walter immediately saw the folly in Gary's plan, but for whatever reason, he decided to go along. After all, how much trouble could he get into merely standing guard at the door?

Armed with pitchforks, the two steeled themselves for battle, and Gary pulled up the edge of the first pallet.

Now feral rats, in most people's way of thinking; with their dark beady eyes, bulbous hairy bodies, long scaly tails, and yellow snapping teeth are not pretty animals at best. They are so abhorrent in fact that many grown men will turn tail and run at the mere sight of a rat, even when properly armed.

Other farm animals will often give a rat the right-of-way as well. Most experienced farm cats will tensely observe a fleeing rat, twitch their tails in excitement, but refuse to give chase. An occasional farm dog may try to deal with a rat—if they can catch it—but a rat is known for being fleet of foot and somewhat vicious—especially if cornered.

Men it seems, sometimes aren't nearly as wise as most common farm animals.

The two men got lucky at first. As Gary lifted one edge of the nearest pallet, a couple of rats scrambled out and began a lightning-fast dash around the inside perimeter of the building. Gary followed in hot pursuit, stabbing at them with his pitchfork as he ran. He soon discovered though, that he wasn't nearly as good with his chosen weapon as he thought he was. He found that trying to stab a fleeing rat with a pitchfork wasn't unlike trying to scoop up shelled sweet peas off his dinner plate with a butter knife.

As the scrambling rodents raced frantically ahead of the man with the slashing pitchfork, they saw the sun-lit door in the otherwise semi-dark interior of the building. Seeing freedom in their near future, they made a mad dash straight for where Walter was standing guard in the doorway. The grown man's legs instantly began dancing like a puppet on a string while he screamed like a woman and slammed the flat of his pitchfork down over and over again on the pallets in front of him. Fortunately, the rats retreated—that time.

After several futile attempts to dispatch the rats with a pitchfork, the two decided that a much more effective weapon would be an irrigation shovel. Such a fine weapon could be used to smash said fleeing rodent, or if thrust with enough speed and accuracy, could possibly cleave the rat in two.

Emboldened now by his new weapon, Gary moved the second pallet. Several large speeding rats broke away at the same time.

Consider now that even if rats may not have a lot of cognitive thought, they do have a strong instinct for either fight or flight.

Walter was the only thing standing between the rats and freedom. They charged!

Down came Walter's shovel, flat on the pallets in front of the determined wave of scrambling rats. The concussion from the shovel blow on the wooden pallets raised a blinding puff of powdered calf feed and turned the fleeing rats around. Now Gary stood firmly between them and escape.

Before Gary could swing his shovel, the rats evidently realized that there was no safety on the ground floor, and when they spotted a couple of denim-clad legs, leading like Jack's immortal beanstalk into the dim light above them, up the man's pant legs, they dashed.

Now It was Gary's turn to scream like a woman, run in place, and thrash wildly at his pants legs with his gloved hands. It was a good thing Walter was out of shovel range at this point, or Walter's shovel may have critically injured Gary as he tried to assist.

Out of breath, and panting both from exertion and fear, both men quickly retreated through the rough-cut opening to re-think what they thought had seemed like such fun only a few minutes before.

Across the room, the rats that had escaped the shovels and slipped safely beneath the pallets again waited for the men's next move.

Both men knew that defeat was not an option. Walking away without a decisive victory over a bunch of silly rats would sully their good names forever. Their tales of terror would undoubtedly result in howls of laughter every time their story was told, embellished, and then re-told by their fellow farmhands.

The two considered using fire but knew that option would destroy the building, and possibly set the rest of the barnyard ablaze as torrents of flaming rats poured through the opening trying to escape the roaring flames.

Poison would take too long, and water would simply flush them out of the bin—wet and angry—but unharmed.

It took a while, but eventually, the two realized that they couldn't simply walk away from the battle they had begun. They had to re-enter the fray.

Somewhat driven now by a sense of urgency and the fear of ridicule, they gathered up what fresh courage they could, and sneaked dutifully back into the lion's (rat's) den. Somewhat wiser now; rather than aggressively beginning the next skirmish by lifting a whole pallet, and dislodging half a dozen rats at a time, Gary would simply jiggle or pound on a pallet until one or sometimes two rats would begin their merry-go-round race for freedom around the perimeter of the steel building.

After a long, laborious, and often panic-stricken battle, the two reluctant heroes eventually wrought a hard-fought victory and vanquished every foe.

Exhausted, pale-faced, and drenched in sweat; the two men stepped outside and leaned heavily against the old granary while they breathed in a few deep cleansing breaths of fresh barnyard air. Neither spoke for a long time.

"Someday we're going to look back on this and laugh," Gary finally managed.

"Maybe," Walter said dubiously. "Meanwhile I know I'm going to have nightmares for months."

"I promise I won't tell anybody you can scream like a woman," Gary snickered.

Walter simply offered a tired smile. "Ditto," he said.

Chickenpox
Alice M Batzel

When our first child was three years old, I was eager to plan playdates where I could exchange an hour or two with other moms and our children could gain some social skills by playing together, learning how to share, and adjusting to brief separation from mom without an emotional nuclear meltdown. I looked forward to the playdates as much as my son, and during some hectic weeks, I longed for that play date. On one such day, I was terribly disappointed. Little Scotty Shirts could not come to our home…he had the chickenpox. It was terrible for little red-haired Scotty, and emotionally disappointing for me because my son needed a playmate so that I could accomplish a few projects with minimal supervision of the little tots playing together. We managed to get through that day, and when my husband got home from work, I told him all about poor Scotty Shirts getting the chickenpox, how he had to stay away from other children because he was fevering and contagious, and our son missed playing with his little pal. The topic of chickenpox was in our home daily for three weeks while Scotty Shirts had to miss the playdates.

As the days passed and Scotty Shirts continued to be absent from our home, one day my three-year-old son asked, "Can Scotty come and play today, or does he still have the snapplecraps?" At that question, my husband and I immediately looked at each other with an inquisitive expression.

"What did he say?" my husband whispered to me.

"Let's ask him to repeat that," I replied. We asked our son to tell us again what he had said so that we could be sure of exactly what he asked us.

With innocence, he immediately said, "Can Scotty come and play today, or does he still have the snapplecraps?"

My husband and I looked at each other and said in unison, "The snapplecraps? What's that? I haven't heard of that before."

Our son replied, "Scotty has been sick with the snapplecraps for a long time, and I want him to come and play with me."

My husband and I looked at each other again, and as if a lightbulb simultaneously came on above each of our heads, we realized that to our son, the strange word of chickenpox could have easily been thought of as snapplecraps. We tried to suppress any laughter and seriously answered our son's question.

"Scotty is getting better, but he still has a little bit of the chickenpox; maybe next week he'll be well enough that he can come over to play."

Our son readily accepted that response, yet, my husband and I were still trying to suppress any laughter about the new word our little son had introduced into our vocabulary.

Over the ensuing years, when our children experienced the dreaded childhood disease of chickenpox, they looked like lepers with the abundant scabs that it temporarily produced. It required vigilant care, and with more than one child at a time experiencing it in our household, I thought we would never see the end of it. During that saga, my husband and I would speak of it with the correct medical terminology when speaking to the children, but when we were alone, you can be sure we referred to it as the snapplecraps.

It's been over 40 years since and, thankfully, a vaccine is now available which gives a great deal of protection to children against that viral illness. Nevertheless, occasionally we'll hear that someone has the chickenpox, and without hesitation, I think to myself…Oh, surely, you must mean the snapplecraps, and I find myself giggling still.

The Reverence Dog of Thurber Ward

Steve Odenthal

Bicknell is a quiet place, a spec along a road that winds down into canyons, narrows, and onward to amazing vacation memories. The town is a gem, not fully dusted off by most passers-by driving toward a scheduled adventure but given a bit of time it has its own very special glow. Those with a true heritage in this area never quite move fully away. My wife, Valerie, for example, hails from the Mangum line of Wayne County. Throughout her childhood, she never missed an opportunity to visit her grandparents, Clifford and Beth's home. More importantly, my wife instilled in the next generation, her children, a love for the serene and peaceful life available in this place that captures time and quiets hearts.

Bicknell, founded (more or less) in 1879 in its current location, was then known as Thurber— named for A.K. Thurber who built the first homestead in the area. The little town of Thurber, if it had any claim to fame at all in those days, stood stoically as a Gateway to the fabulous Wayne Wonderland—better known now as Capitol Reef. Like the red and stony National Park down the road, the people of Bicknell, all 387 (on a good day), are strong and reserved by nature. Farming and ranching are the names of the game here, with a mix of logging and lumber helping to make ends meet for those families that call this hard paradise home. God's hand is everywhere in the design, from the sandstone and red rock formations to the hard desert soil, a clay that hosts crop until harvest between the flash floods which frequent the valley. Bicknell is a chores-first community, with its inhabitants secure in a shared but unspoken belief that God loves a good hike, and, with a faithful dog and walking stick at his side, this place is where the big man chooses to stroll. There have been sightings.

To say that the residents of Bicknell love their dogs is akin to saying that their sky is blue. It is. Vibrantly so, in between the quick, sudden, and dramatic summer storms and the winter blizzards that try in vain to hide the magnificence of the Almighty's red cliff-ed motifs. That is not to say that a visitor like you, or me for that matter, notice the town's tail-waggers while passing through or even hears them at night after booking a room at the Aquarius or SunGlow motel. From the time they were pups, these family members have been raised to be purposeful, loyal, and silent. These four-legged citizens go about their business, each having their own routes and chores—you are merely a distraction to pay a short second of attention to. Each Lab, Collie, or Shepard emulates his owner's countenance in this way. If you see them at all, it will likely be in the back of a pick-up, heading to a job or a lake, or perhaps lying in a bit of shade but still on duty, watching you back. Nod at them, offer a "Hey, boy" and you will get in return a small head bob as they eye you calmly, not skittish at all. Bicknell is theirs, and you are either a traveler on the way to an adventure down the highway or one of the unfortunate, heading back up to the grind and away from the town's quiet lifestyle. State Route 24, the single-lane highway that serves as Main Street offers only these two options and these four-legged guardians of the town know it.

Bicknell is a town that understands its place in the scheme of things. The terms over to, up ta, down at, the bottoms and Boulder are directional compass points to the locals. They like to fish, although chores always do come first. Places like Lower Bounds and Forsythe are known by locals and visitors as well, but word is swift and sure among the residents of where the catching is good at any minute of the day. Ask, and you will always get a twinkle-eyed reply, complete with "up ta" directions. Sometimes, they will let you in on the latest, but not always. It may depend on their afternoon plans. However, you can count on that twinkle in their eye and their own particular version of a smile.

Bicknell also is a place where people know their individual plans and routines throughout the week. Come Sunday in this community there are those that sit in congregations in a couple of different assembly places, and there are those who don't. Most from around these parts know which plan is theirs from years of practice. Rarely is an eyebrow raised or a new threshold crossed on these mornings as the Bicknell townsfolk go about their own version of worship. But, should visitors arrive as our family did one Sunday, word passes quickly, and an association is made tying the strangers into the greater Thurber-Bicknell family.

"Oh, yes. That's Clifford's granddaughter and her family."

"Which one is she?"

"I think that's Claudia's oldest daughter."

"That's little Jiminy? That's what Cula used to call her—on account of how tiny she was as a child. Little Jiminy Cricket, well, I'll be."

Cula Ekker was somewhat world renown for her Pickle Pie served at the Sunglow Café on Main Street. It is still worth the stop, by the way. You will never leave hungry. If Cula took a shining to you, you might have a new nickname. She was direct like that. And her culinary delights like Pinto Bean, Oatmeal, Buttermilk, and Pickle Pie made her a celebrity chef in her own right. A favorable nickname from Cula was a badge of honor in this community.

"Well then, is Claudia down ta visit, as well?"

"She'd be here if she was. Don't see her, though."

And such was the talk as our little family joined the Thurber Ward services. Why Thurber and not Bicknell Ward, you ask? Tradition. When the Ward organized it adopted the proper town name as was the Church of Jesus Christ of Latter-Day Saint tradition. Many years later, Thomas Bicknell, an educator from Rhode Island, offered to donate 500 books for a library to any Utah town that officially took his name. In 1916 the name change became official for the town but not for the Ward that assembled there. Sounds suspiciously like a Broadway show of some notoriety, but I am assured that is just coincidence. You won't find a lot of dancing and breaking into song in this town—remember stoic and traditional comes naturally to these unruffled, salt-of-the-earth residents.

We took our seats in the chapel with the Thurber Ward members, careful to not take up an unofficially-officially assigned bench seat. (Even in the larger cities and towns of Utah squatters' rights to specific pews can be a thing.) After we settled in and validated our count of children with the number we had loaded in the car, we enjoyed the quiet and reverence that accompanied the prelude organ music. Looking around the congregation, all was in order and not a hair out of place of those members not follicle challenged. Ties were done up, and a new shine was on the shoes of all the gathered Thurber-ites. Not so much with my own troop of visitors, but we at least had headed in that fashion direction.

After a smile and a welcome from the pulpit, the parishioners erupted in song sweeping us up in the gravelly flow. We fit right in and gave our best voice to the effort as the meeting began in earnest. In short order, the bread of the Sacrament was prepared, blessed, and delivered to the congregation by solemn Deacons on silver trays. The administration of the ordinance was deliberate and dignified; every care was made to ensure that no one in the hallway had been missed.

Next came the water portion of the Sacrament which the same Deacons delivered to the pews. As the assembled worshipers sat in reverence, waiting for the tray to reach them so that they could partake, a large and well-combed Yellow Labrador entered the front of the chapel.

The dog quietly fell in line three paces behind the Deacon administering the sacramental water, matching the young man's stops at each pew. The canine watched each member of the congregation take their sip and seemed to be approving each individual's swallow.

From our seats in the back row of the chapel, my family had an unobstructed view of this unexpected, but well-behaved intruder. I must say he was every bit as reverent as anyone in the building. It amazed us that no one stirred, made a fuss, or moved to leash the animal.

As the Deacon completed his rounds, he made his way back up to the Sacrament table. Meanwhile, the Lab stood stoically at the back of the chapel looking up toward the pulpit. The Bishop rose and approached the microphone.

"Has everyone received the opportunity to partake of the Sacrament?"

It appeared that everyone had received the emblems of the Sacrament. As the Bishop gazed out at the congregation, I am sure that his eyes met those of the Yellow Lab in the back corner of the Chapel. I witnessed the Lab nod his head slightly to acknowledge the Bishop at that moment, and then the majestic dog moved out the doors held open by two reverent young men.

"Thank you." The Bishop sat back down, and the Deacons and Teachers dispersed, allowing the rest of the meeting to continue.

After the meetings of the day, we mingled among the members and renewed acquaintances and traced family trees. Jiminy, I mean, Valerie recounted tales and reconnected with memories right and left. I sought out the Bishop and the Lab.

"I notice that you had a visitor for the Sacrament. Does he attend often?"

"We've seen him around town from time to time." The Bishop smiled. "Especially on nice days like this. His owner likes to hike. They check in, now and again."

With that, a tug on his elbow turned the Bishop's focus to a Deacon who needed him. I wandered off to find my family. In my search, I passed a group of boys checking out a large walking stick propped against the wall.

"Careful, boys. Someone is coming back for that."

They looked back at me in silence for a moment and then continued their study.

I found Val and the gang, and we started back up State Route 24, back to the grind. We speak now and then about Bicknell and our favorite memories there. While the town can boast of the fastest parade in America (55 MPH between Torrey and Bicknell), the Bicknell International Film Festival *Better Living Through Bad Cinema* and unbelievably gorgeous scenery, the Reverence Dog of Thurber Ward must rank high upon our list of favorite memories.

We will be back. It's in Jiminy 's blood—and now mine as well.

Raising Kids

Josie Hulme

We tore down our house the beginning of July before the ink had even dried on the stamped plans. "It'll be three weeks, babe," I assured my reluctant husband. He's from California where the only tools needed to fix something are Google and a credit card. My pioneer do-it-yourself attitude has been an adjustment for him—he's still adjusting after twenty years. Added to that, I'm a dyed-in-the-wool, head-in-the-sky Pollyanna and his feet are firmly planted in the manure-rich soil of reality. He knew from past experience that "three weeks" was going to be a lot longer.

Ever since we bought our house sixteen years ago, we've had a vision of what it could become. I fell in love with the little brick home the first time I saw it. The Garners built it almost one hundred fifty years ago—it's the oldest house in the neighborhood. It's seen births and deaths, tears of happiness and tears of sorrow, and it's provided a safe-haven for generations of families just like mine. The original brick house has been added to in the '50s and again in the '60s, and eight years ago, we added our own five-bedroom/two bath addition. Now it was time to complete that sixteen-year-old vision.

The first hurdle we faced was building codes. Nothing was up to code except our most recent addition. Anything we wanted to build a second story on had to be torn down to the dirt and rebuilt. I declared it a sacrilege to tear down the original brick home, but I had no such qualms about the poorly constructed '50s and '60s additions. Of course, losing this portion of the house meant no kitchen, no laundry room, and no bathroom, but we could do anything for three weeks, right?

I came away from the teardown with one smashed fingernail.

Everyone else wasn't so lucky. My husband had a bloody head, a nail through his foot, scraped up arms from falling down a hole in the dark, and a spectacular bruise on his thigh from tripping over a pipe. Between our five children, there were two bloody shins, a hole in a foot, one "I'm sure it's broken, Mom" thumb, three smashed fingers, two tumbles down the ladder, and a partridge in a pear tree.

Not everything was bad, though. Friends and neighbors came to help. We kept a cooler full of ice-cold sodas and a freezer stocked with every ice cream bar known to man and passed these out liberally to everyone who labored. Parents enthusiastically sent their children to help at our tuition-free Hard Work University and, with the bribe of sodas and ice cream, they came in droves.

Canvas garages sprouted in our yard seemingly overnight to house the displaced items: washing machines, cabinets, dishwashers, mowers, doors, windows, even a toilet was wedged between the furnace and the water heater. The grass we were too busy to mow grew long and died in the scorching summer heat, laying its stiff, brown body over small items that hadn't found a home yet: bungee cords, bricks, crowbars, iron pipes and shelf brackets—things I'm sure I'll need before I find them next spring when I run over them with my mower.

It took a week to tear down and haul away the old house. I hid my smirk from my husband. We were right on schedule. Then came the only outside help I planned to hire: the foundation guys. And that's where my schedule fell apart.

Contractors and builders live in an alternate reality. Time means something different to them than it does to the rest of us. It's like they have a secret oath they take when they get their license: I solemnly promise to never finish on time, to be late for every deadline, and to not show up for days at a time, and this I do with the understanding that as we all adhere to this code, our clients will complain, but there will be nothing they can do about it. Amen.

Two weeks later, they still weren't finished. A week after that, all the concrete had been poured, but a few odds and ends still needed to be touched up. I tried to convince my husband to unclench his teeth since we couldn't build anyway because the lumber yard had messed up our order and our lumber hadn't come in yet. He acknowledged the veracity of my statement, but his jaw stayed bunched. I think he was mad at the lumberyard, too.

Meanwhile, navigating my house looked something like this: come in the front door, skirt the pile of tools sprawling all over the living room, open a newly-added door to what used to be the kitchen and is now the outside, climb down a short ladder, traverse the uneven dirt, walk up a step stool, cross over an exposed sewer pipe, down another step stool, across more dirt, then up a short ladder to enter the downstairs bedrooms or up a tall ladder to enter the upstairs bedrooms. Needless to say, we thought long and hard about what we might be forgetting in the room we were about to leave before we made this trek.

The day our lumber came in and we put a floor across that empty space eliminating the need for all but one ladder, my daughter said, "I never knew how happy two flat boards could make me. This is the most excited I will ever be!" She's a teenager, so the next 'most exciting' thing will be next weekend, but her words were still true. During the Ladder Trial of '18, we learned to appreciate floors—a part of the house we had simply walked across and never thought of before except to complain when we had to sweep or vacuum them. They meant something different now.

When I was a young girl, my family added on to our house like it was an abacus—every year another addition. My dad always said, "I'm not building a house; I'm raising kids." I've found that statement to be true myself. As much hassle as this has been for the last three months—and it's nowhere near finished yet—it's been delightful to see my kids work even when they don't want to, to learn how to run tools they never even knew existed, to see them sit back after a hard day's work and look at what their labor produced, and say, "This is good."

The Paddock

James D Beers

Scoot stood up from his seat on the log and threw a piece of birch on the flickering campfire, a tiny flame in the darkening forest.

"There you have it," he said, watching the birch bark curl and light. "That's why the Wendigo still roams these parts, searching for lone hunters, hikers, and campers."

"Good one, Scoot," Hank piped in through a mouthful of s'more. "'cept you've told it at every campfire since Scout Camp twenty-five years ago."

Jack, Verl, and I chuckled, each of us at various stages of making and eating s'mores.

"Camp Willahitchee! I totally remember that!" Verl plucked the roasted marshmallow from his stick, smiling and reminiscing.

"Yeah, tell us a different one," Jack said.

"But that one's a classic," Scoot said, returning to his spot on the log next to Hank. "Don't tell me none of you ever think about the Wendigo when you're out hikin' and huntin'. I know better."

I stuffed the last corner of a s'more into my mouth. "Not me, Scoot," I said, graham cracker crumbs spilling out over my lips. "I think of Bigfoot."

"Oh, no! Not another Bigfoot story."

Hank thought Bigfoot was a crock of hooey, and he let us all know last year when my Bigfoot yarn spurred Verl, Jack, and Scoot to add their own Bigfoot narratives. "Someone come up with a different one."

"Fine! Why don't you tell one, Hank?" I said. "I'm thinking—"

"How 'bout the Golden Arm?" Scoot interrupted.

"Come on, dude!" Jack was already roasting another marshmallow for another s'more. "Everybody knows that one. And it ain't scary."

"While you're thinking, Hank, why don't we hear one from Verl?" I said. "You never tell any ghost stories, Verl. Surely you've got some."

Other than the one about Bigfoot the year before, I couldn't think of another time in the last ten years of our annual campout when Verl had shared any tales.

"Yeah, Verl. Why don't you tell one?" Hank tried to divert any attention from his turn further.

Verl didn't respond; he sat there gazing into the fire, deep in thought. No one said a word, waiting for Verl to speak up. For a moment, the only sound was the crackle of our small fire and the thrum of crickets chirping in the meadow. Then Verl spoke, his voice serious, the look on his face one of repressed fear.

"Years ago, when I was a teenager, I took a date to the Hogle Zoo in Salt Lake City. It was June 15, 1993, a day that will live in infamy throughout zoo history. Even now I cringe in horror at what happened, of what the other visitors and we saw and experienced that summer afternoon—"

"What? Did you try to kiss her and she Kung-fu'd you in public?" Scoot needled, smiling and chuckling.

"SHHH!" I told Scoot.

The mood had already been set, and Jack, Hank, and I hunkered closer to the fire to hear Verl's story. Scoot quit chuckling and reflexively joined us.

"Something—maybe the heat, maybe some misalignment with the moon—disturbed the atmosphere that day, forming a palpable uneasiness across the zoo," Verl continued. "We were making our way to the gorilla exhibit when a lion roared in the distance. My date gasped and clung to me as if I were Alan Quartermain, her only hope in an urban-surrounded jungle. From my curled toes to the goosepimpled hair follicles, on the top of my head, I knew something was about to happen—"

I took a quick look at Hank, Scoot, and Jack, wondering if they were thinking the same thing I was—surely Verl was about to tell us that a man-eating lion had managed to break through display glass and maul some poor onlookers. Or maybe a male silverback gorilla with a penchant for tearing off people's arms had escaped and carried a screaming lady to the top of a zoo tree.

"I felt it in my bones," Verl gulped, "and, as we walked around, I could tell that the animals also felt it. The male silverback beat his chest several times, a black bear paced about its hold, gazelles galloped across their simulated savannah, and monkeys swung around their enclosures. Even the sloths were on the move. Worst of all was how the male lion looked at me through the display glass. Our eyes connected, and I heard him say in my mind, I could kill you and eat you for breakfast."

Call me crazy, but what Verl was describing sounded like fairly normal animal behavior. Perhaps the animals at the Hogle Zoo are generally lazier than the average zoo animal? I was dubious. Nevertheless, I stayed perched on the edge of the log seat, transfixed with Verl's retelling. The other guys hadn't even blinked.

"Around 4:00 p.m., I bought us a couple of ice cream cones to eat as we visited the exhibits."

The tension in Verl's voice felt like it was going to snap, and all hell would break loose. Hank, Scoot, Jack, and I were certain Verl was about to reveal a blood-and-guts climax.

"We slowly made our way to the hippo paddock, a building of nightmares and the birthplace of my teenage PTSD."

Hippos! I should have known! They're the most dangerous animal in Africa, or so I'd read. Every year entire African tribes are wiped out by marauding hippos. Safari guides claim they'll bite a boat in half and chew any passengers to death. I've heard they have tusks the size of Kong and weigh more than a car. Verl's story could not end well—an escaped hippo could've killed millions! Perhaps a hippo got loose and squished his date. I didn't know, but my mind was racing with the possibilities.

"The paddock was full of people who wanted to see the hippos and escape the hot sun. My date and I walked up to the belly-high glass barrier overlooking an enormous tank of water. A couple of penguins were swimming around on the surface, and a huge hippo walked along the bottom. We watched for a couple of minutes. Bubbles erupted sporadically from the giant's underwater head before the massive beast made its way out of the tank and onto a concrete beach. He, she, whatever it was, wasn't on the concrete beach for thirty seconds before—" Verl paused, shuddered, and again stared blankly into the fire.

"What?! What happened?" Jack pleaded.

I couldn't stop my mind from seeing a bulbous hippo leaping off the concrete beach, crashing through the glass barrier, and munching all the visitors to ribbons except for Verl. Verl would've been the only one to escape, and he must've suffered years of survivor's guilt. No wonder he never spoke of this.

"Dude, what happened?" Scoot asked, still on the edge of the log seat.

"Yeah, tell us," said Hank.

Verl cleared his throat and continued with his story, his lower lip quivering. "The beast started rapidly wagging its fat, wicked tail like a caffeinated Weiner dog excited to see its master. Then it pooped."

From the corners of my fear-widened eyes, I watched Scoot's jaw drop and eyes bug out, and Jack drop his roasting stick—marshmallow and all—on the ground.

"Fecal shrapnel exploded all over the paddock. Instinctively I dropped my ice cream cone over the barrier into the tank and then tackled my date to the ground, trying to protect her from the blast. 'Holy crap!' she yelled, stealing the words right out of my mouth. Lying there, my date next to me, I made a quick look around the paddock. People were shielding their babies in strollers, others were hunkered down against the glass barrier, and still, others were stampeding the exits, their clothes speckled with poo spackle. The air above us was awash with flying dung flecks, some of them descending on us like bombs from a fetid blitzkrieg."

What was I hearing? My mind, my body, with all the adrenaline pumping through it, had been prepared for blood and carnage. But Verl's story was horrifying! All I could think of was Morrison's 1937 broadcast of the Hindenburg crash: "Oh, the humanity!"

"All of a sudden everything slowed down as if life were in slow motion," Verl continued, still staring into the fire, lip quivering. "I looked through the barrier glass and could see the hippo's swishing tail. In my mind's eye, every swish was synchronized to the cannon shots at the end of Tchaikovsky's 1812 Overture now playing in my head. 'Run!' I yelled at my date. She got up and ran, leaving her poo-shot ice cream cone on the paddock floor. I followed her out the entrance, emerging from the building just as a troop of hippo trainers carrying riot shields went racing in to check for survivors.

"Outside, the gathered crowd was a mass of chaos— people recounting the tale to other zoo visitors, families staring blankly ahead while zoo officials tried to wipe off the muck, babies, and children crying. It was horrible! Shortly, a zookeeper handed us a roll of paper towels and a spray bottle of water. We cleaned off as well as we could, and then I drove us home. We never spoke of the event again."

Verl continued staring into the fire, lost in the traumatic memory. The rest of us sat there, mouths agape, wondering at the tale just told.

Two, maybe three minutes passed in silence before Hank made the first sound. A chuckle rumbled from his gut and out his mouth and nose. Scoot followed with a few snickering snorts, and then Jack heartily laughed. I couldn't help myself; I joined in the laughter. What had been a tensely told, horrifying experience now seemed ridiculously funny.

"Hippo poop!" Hank yelled between gasping belts of laughter. "Shielding babies! HAAA!" Jack cried, wiping tears with one hand and rubbing his laughed-over gut with the other. "Riot shields!" Scoot could barely get the words out, falling off his log seat and rolling on the ground laughing.

"Man!" I grabbed Verl by the shoulder, trying to support myself through the gut-wrenching giggles. "I thought . . . HAAA! I thought you were gonna—HA! HAAA! . . . Tell us about an escaped animal. HA! HA! That was way better! HAAA!"

Verl chuckled lightly and added, "I guess it is kind of funny when you think about it. Hippo poop—HA!" Pretty soon, Verl was laughing along with us.

"Did you ever take the girl out again?" Jack asked between laughing gasps.

"Nope. She married my cousin. The funny thing is, he's the Hogle Zoo veterinarian! HAAA!"

Please Don't Stop the Music

Jared Quan

Looking around the electronics department of the Wal-Mart, I let out a long deep sigh. It was getting close to the end of a long workday, and I had finally finished sorting the returns. I started my slow saunter through the department in orbit opposite the other two associates in the department.

"Hey," Assistant Manager Rachael said, waving me over. Her short five-foot-two frame was nearly hidden by the video display feature on the end cap.

"Sup," I said. I often dreaded the call of a manager so close to knocking off and feared the worse.

"I need you to figure out how to get rid of all this open box stuff,"

"Sure thing, do you want me to use the trash compactor, or hide it in another department," I joked.

Though this was a joke, I knew for a fact that some perfectly good items were tossed into the trash compactor per contractual agreements depending on circumstance.

"No, no, we need to get this stuff sold, the district manager is coming tomorrow, and I will get killed if the electronics department has all this stuff laying around,"

"What if we set it up near the front-end registers, and ran some power to it?"

"I don't know; we would need to have an associate always manning it,"

"Steven and I can man it, we will get this sold for you," Steven was one of the few people to take me under his wing when I started, so I knew that he had my back if I decided to do something crazy.

Reminiscent of the time we strung speaker wire up into the ceiling using the scissor lift so people walking through the isle could experience full surround sound.

"I will approve it this time, but don't let me down,"

I shrugged, "worst-case scenario we are in the same place we are now."

Heather gave me a serious look, "No, really, do whatever you have to get rid of it."

"Yes, Ma'am," I said with a sharp salute. Convincing management to sign off on stuff was half the battle, I would face more challenges before I could get this running.

Heather walked away with the radio chirping in her ear. Looking around the department, I found Steven "adjusting" the TV's where the demo movie was playing.

"Hey, we have an assignment," I said.

"Yup, I heard, and it won't work," Steven said, refusing to look at me. This was his typical nonchalant greeting.

"You have to admit it is better than sitting back here, plus I have something special in mind," I said with a devious grin.

A thoughtful look came over his face before he turned his six-foot-one frame towards me. "Whatcha got in mind?"

"Just go get two tables set up just in front of the clothes facing the registers," I said.

"You're not going to get us fired, right?"

"I am ninety percent sure, we will be fine," I was more like fifty percent sure we weren't going to get into trouble.

"That's good enough for government work; I will see you upfront," I started loading up a tall cart with all the open box items. I went out of my way to put the massive seven speakers surround sound and its accompanying subwoofer onto the cart.

"And where do you think you are taking that?" Alan, the department manager, asked. One of the obstacles I knew I would eventually have to face.

"Heather approved for me to take this upfront and get rid of this stuff," I said.

"Funny, she didn't say anything to me about it," Alan said. He scrunched up his nose and tilted his head back to offer me a suspicious look through his thick black-framed glasses.

"We only have a couple of hours before we are off, so I need to get this upfront," I said cheerfully. I knew Alan had the power to shut down my show; he would just go up a level in management, and most likely would if he thought I would make him look bad in any way.

"Okay, but if I hear this wasn't approved, then I am going to make sure you get written up,"

I offer him a quick thumb up and a wink as I pulled the cart to the front of the store. As planned, Steven had the two tables set up. It was perfectly placed, nearly dead center with the row of registers across the way.

"So, what's the plan, that will eventually fail?" Steven asked.

"Go grab an extension cord, and I will start setting up," I said.

"That's good; I will be able to say I was following orders,"

"Oh, and grab a couple of CDs', something with some dance mixes."

"And I forgot to bring my DJ headphones and glasses," He said sarcastically. Steven let out a laugh as he turned to fulfill the request.

I felt like we were past the point of no return, so we needed to go all-in on this. As expected, the Customer Service Manager made her way over to the table filled with electronics.

"So, what are you doing?" Gina asked. Her signature brown hair bob and reading glasses seemed more curious than threatened.

"We are going to be providing tonight's entertainment," I said with a big smile.

"You are trouble; you know that?" She asked, "Just don't interfere with the registers."

"You got it," I said.

Steven arrived just in time with the cord and a stack of CDs. As requested, he brought a solid offering of dance mixes. After a moment, everything powered up, and we were in business.

"Let's start low and ease them into it," I said.

"Here, I will let you put it in and let you pick the disc to get us started, that way none of my fingerprints will be on here for evidence,"

"Good to know we are in this together,"

He raised his hands, "it is your show, boss."

I rolled my eyes and put the first CD into the player. I left the volume at a very comfortable level, as the first songs played.

I got nervous as the Store Manager approached surrounded by the co-managers and assistant managers.

"Who approved this one?" Store Manager Mike asked. Time seemed to stand still for a moment as no one seemed to say anything, and I didn't see Heather in the group at first.

"I did," Heather said from the back of the group.

"Good work, way to think outside the box," He said.

"Thank you," She said.

"Just don't turn it up too loud boys," He said. The group continued on its way.

My heart finally started beating again after the mini panic attack. I glanced back to see that Steven had taken a couple of steps back into the

77

clothes to hide from the group.

"What are you doing?" I asked.

"Nothing?" He shrugged.

"Get over here; I need you to walk over to the registers to make sure we have the speakers pointed for maximum effect,"

"Sir, yes sir,"

After a few minutes of tinkering and testing, we felt satisfied with the speaker position and then went onto adjusting the bass and treble settings.

"So, what is our excuse when management comes back up here to yell at us for turning the music up too loud?"

"I figure in five more minutes management will be safely back in the HR office having their final meeting of the night, and we will have thirty minutes," I was, of course, making up all the numbers I was spouting.

Once again, he held his hands up in a surrendering position, "Whatever you say, sir."

We watched the clock carefully, and right at the five-minute mark, I slid in the harder dance mix. The first song went on, and I turned the volume up a couple of notches. To be perfectly honest, I was expecting to get shut down right then, but neither management or customers seemed to notice the music or volume change.

"Disappointing," Steven said.

"Just wait," I said.

The next song came on, and I turned the volume up much louder, which drew looks, and even a glance from the Customer Service Manager. However, once again, no one shut us down, and no one complained.

"Yet again, disappointing," Steven said.

"This is going to be the one," I said. Steven had to know at this point that I had no idea what would happen next.

The next song started up, and I turned the volume all the way up to the point where it almost distorted. The deep thump of the lead into the Rihanna song 'Please Don't Stop the Music' could be felt and heard in every corner of the store now.

Everyone started dancing. I watched as the cashiers, the customers, and even the Customer service manager were all dancing. The song really started to get going we found ourselves suddenly with twenty-five teenagers dancing right in front of the table in a flash mob. I looked around to see customers in every department within sight dancing and many singing along. People walking into the store instantly started joining in. Everyone was smiling ear to ear as they got into it.

I managed to catch a glimpse of department manager Alan dancing. As the song neared its end, we reached a critical mass of people in front of the table with nearly thirty people dancing next to each other like a club. Then the song ended. I looked over to see the Customer Service manager wave a warning, and I powered down the system.

There was a collective "awe."

Right on time, the whole management team arrives back at the table.

"How loud…" Mike started to ask. He is interrupted by a customer.

"I would like to buy that system," The customer said.

"Sure thing let's get that loaded up for you," Steven promptly said.

Mike moved to get closer to me when he was interrupted by another customer.

"Does that system sound like the one that was just playing?" The customer pointed to a second system on the table.

"Yes, sir," I said.

"Then I will take it," He replied.

"I guess—good work?" Mike said, "Just don't do that again."

"You got it, boss," I said.

The management team started to walk away again when Heather offered a high five as she walked past the table.

"You know, I can't believe that worked," Steven said as he returned to the table.

"Never underestimate the power of loud music," I said.

For nearly six minutes, the entire Wal-Mart store customers to employees were in perfect harmony. No one ever complained about it, and many customers and employees asked several times over the next few weeks when we were going to play music like that again. Unfortunately, it never happened.

One and Done

Dave Willes

As a general rule, I don't ever stretch myself too far out of my comfort zone. You know, it's just too...uncomfortable. Had I been born in medieval times, I'm sure I would have been a bookbinder, or shoemaker, or (heaven forbid) rat catcher to the King. But certainly nothing overly taxing or adventurous.

I received my bachelor's degree at BYU in 1981 and got a job offer from Exxon Corp that was just too good to pass up—great starting wage, lots of things to do, and good potential for career growth. Computers were starting to perform the mundane activities of accounting, and my boss was expecting me to help automate modules to speed up the return on results. Sounds like fun, right? The only problem was we were in Texas, and the rest of our family was in Idaho and Utah, and my wife was especially homesick.

Jana and I really enjoyed the people in Houston, although our first apartment was a little scary. But we soon found a condo in a new area and thought we might be able to make a go of it, at least for a few years while I got some experience. We figured a 3 or 4-year stint in Houston would be great, and then off to greater and better things. So, we set out to discover Texas.

Coming from the cloistered confines of BYU, we were little prepared for the alien nature of our new surroundings. Our first domicile was in a condominium. As we were led through the apartment by the real estate agent, Jana was observing the bugs on the walls. She inquired as gracefully as she could, "I don't mean to be nosy, but do you have a bug problem in these apartments?" The agent just leaned back and laughed, "Honey, welcome to Houston!"

Welcome to Houston, indeed! If you have roaches in Utah, you have a bug problem. Call an exterminator and move on. When you have roaches in Texas, you saddle up and ride!

Once, Jana woke me up in the middle of the night. She quietly whispered that she thought someone was trying to break into our apartment. I grabbed my trusty hammer and proceeded through the darkened house towards a loud, flapping noise in the guest bathroom. Once there, I threw on the lights, only to find an extremely large tree roach lying on its back in the tub, trying to turn himself over. He never got the chance. I drowned him in a pool of bug spray 3 inches deep. He never knew what hit him.

And then there were fire ants. I discovered just how painful fire ant bites were when I was bitten on my arm, and it became swollen and feverish. Extremely painful! And they are ugly, *REALLY* ugly.

But the people of Texas! They were great and friendly and very welcoming. We made a lot of friends there, and it was difficult to leave them when it came time.

✻✻✻

In 1985, our family moved back to Utah when I accepted a finance position on the Space Shuttle Program. I worked for Thiokol, Morton Thiokol, Cordant Technologies, Alliant Techsystems, ATK Launch Group, and Orbital ATK, all while sitting in the same chair. (I'm sure I didn't get all of the names.)

In reality, I worked 30+ years for the same company—without ever leaving the promontory facility. It was a good run.

So, you can tell, I am not the adventurous type. I like what I like, and I'm leery of the unknown.

That's why when I decided to trek up to Angel's Landing in Zion National Park a few years ago, I not only thought I had lost my mind, but my wife and family were almost certain of it. Did I mention, I'm afraid of heights?

My son Coulton assured me that I could do it (after all, he had done it multiple times). Did I mention that Coulton is a big-time thrill seeker, and loves the challenge of doing hard things? This hard thing was to be his third or fourth hike to the summit of Angel's Landing, and he was excited to go again. I, on the other hand, am a wimp. I had no idea what lay ahead. He assured me that I could do it and that he would be there to help if I needed it. Hah, Hah, Hah!

On my first attempt to summit Angels Landing a few years earlier, I not only underachieved, but I did not even make it to Walter's Wiggles (yes, it sounds so innocuous, but those wiggles are darned frightening.) Looking down over the valley below, my wife Jana and I were both seized with absolute terror. Way, way, way down below us were tour buses, the size of small ants. Jana and I both realized that we were not only NOT going to see Walter's Wiggles, but we *were* going to wiggle our waggles back down the path slowly (yes, clinging to the side of the wall). It was then that both Jana and I decided that viewing the red rock was most comfortably enjoyed in our nicely air-conditioned tour buses. Back to the lodge, we went, wandering around the narrows and a few soggy ditches pretending they were streams. To keep my spirits up, I bought a slice of pizza and a Coke.

✳✳✳

Fast forward to Saturday, April 14, 2018. I'm not getting any younger. What the crap! It's now or never! I decided that I was going to give it one more college try. The whole family was there in varying stages. My daughter, Natalie, and her kids climbed to Scout Lookout with Jana and waited for a couple of hours, while the rest of us began to climb. Sons-in law Kenny and Nate, Caitlin (my daughter), Coulton, Ashley (Coulton's wife), and I climbed 5,790 feet into the air, supported by chains, good solid hiking boots, and a lot of prayers!

There was one particularly anxious moment when one hiker decided to cross in front of Kenny to get to the other side (somewhere in there is a chicken joke, but it wasn't too funny). The hiker slipped, and for a moment, we thought he might fall, but with some help from the people around him, he was able to regain his balance. It certainly scared all of us, but it all worked out just fine. No harm, no foul, right?

I was grateful that I had my family with me. I know Caitlin was worried, and both she and her husband, Nate, were very protective of me while we made the trek. I was surrounded by my family every step of the way.

Everyone (especially me) breathed a big sigh of relief once we had completed the journey. And once Kenny recovered from his near miss, we were all able to return safely to our loved ones. It was truly a great adventure.

I had a great time with all of those who joined us. What a great experience! What a great family! The Intrepid Six who made the summit found a reward with the view of some the most beautiful red rock in the world. And I truly felt on top of the world. Oh, and yes. For me, this is one and done. I am complete.

Where Do You Hang Your Coat?

Cecelie Costley

Our religion told us to live within our means and instructed us in the aspects of provident living. We had also grown up on the adage, "Use it up, wear it out, make it do or do without," but we had taken that to the limit, and we were getting desperate.

We were living in Salt Lake in a one-bedroom apartment with four children. The children slept in the bedroom while the dining room housed our king-size bed propped up high on cinder blocks to provide needed storage space beneath it. Three times a day, I swapped the bedspread for a tablecloth, pulled up the chairs and voila we dined.

The bank told us we were only qualified for a tiny box (a starter home) in a run down section of the city. We didn't want that. We wanted space and open-air, room for the kids to run free, not a tiny yard and a kitchen window that faced the neighbor's junky carport. But you know what they say, "be careful what you wish for."

What do you do when your finances haven't kept pace with your growing family? You do what others before you have done; you move out of the city, you find a place to homestead where your wits can make up for your lack of wealth, you go back to nature to try and find the simpler life and reconnect with what is really important. Henry David Thoreau went to Walden Pond; we went to the mountains of southern Idaho. Henry went alone. We did it with four children. Henry didn't have a clue what "roughing it" meant.

The house we could afford was adobe brick built in the 1890s, and even in the summer heat, it was cool and dank. We lit a fire in the kitchen fireplace. The dry wood began to flame merrily, but then it started to smoke and make a sort of humming sound. That was followed by a slow drip, drip, drip of yellow ooze. We leaned in closer. I looked at my husband. He looked at me. "Honey?" we asked each other. The bees swarmed out while we ran for cover, slamming the kitchen door behind us.

Humans hadn't occupied the house for some time, but it was far from empty. I had to serve eviction notices to bees and bats, raccoons, wood rats, and snakes. Big snakes! I came down the stairs one day and almost stepped on a giant blow snake that slithered out from under the bottom step and across the living room floor. It paused, gave me the evil eye, shook its tail at me, and then disappeared down a crack.

Indoor plumbing had been added during the 1930s. Added and then apparently forgotten for only cold water ran in the kitchen. I held my cup under the faucet for a delicious drink of our natural spring water. The crystalline stream flowed and then stopped and spluttered and a worm plopped out into my cup. Further investigation revealed that the spring water was collected in an open cement storage tank that allowed drinking access to all of the wildlife in the area before it was piped to us.

There had been a bathroom, but the toilet lay on the floor in pieces, and the sewage line ran directly out to the creek. My conscience was having a little trouble with that arrangement, but there was an outhouse still standing albeit rather cockeyed behind the house. We would use that. Unfortunately, it was full of hornets, and no one willingly bares their behind to a smelly dark hole full of hornets, so we went back to nature in more ways than one, and my children became rather feral that summer.

From sunup to sundown, the children helped us get the house livable by winter. The leaking roof was repaired with aluminum shingles we cut ourselves from the printing plates of the local newspaper, wood was cut, loaded, unloaded and stacked to use in the "new to us" woodstove, and little fingers stuffed insulation into every wall and floor crack. The children were troopers.

As fall approached, I felt guilty that my children hadn't had any excursions or diversions from their work. Oh, they had run free like wild horses, and they had explored and hiked and swam in the creek, but they hadn't had any refined or cultural experiences so necessary for a balanced education. I decided to leave the wild and take them on a field trip around Salt Lake to places I had enjoyed as a child, like the zoo and the natural history museum and the Lion House.

In preparation, I washed their clothes in grandma's wringer washer which I filled with cold water from the hose, plugged into an extension cord and then set it free to do the Agitation (a dance the kids tried to mimic) across the lawn. When the wash cycle ended, I pulled the plug and refilled it with rinse water from the hose. After the rinse, the children took turns doing the daring chore of sending each item through the wringer which tended to take little fingers as eagerly as it took socks, and then I hung each item on the line to dry while I started cleaning the children.

I cut the burrs out of their hair, combed out the snarls and then put them all in the tub. There was no hot water in the house, but we had painted an old water heater black, rigged it on top of the roof and attached a hose that snaked down through the kitchen window and across the floor to deliver hot water via a garden spray nozzle into the bathtub. You had to do this at just the right time during the day because there was no way to mix cold water with the scalding hot solar-heated water, a fact we had learned the hard way. I squirted and scrubbed and took off the dirty sunbaked top layer of skin on each child. When I thought they looked quite presentable, I loaded them into our hand-me-down pink 1964 Studebaker and headed south for one last summer hoorah in Salt Lake City.

The children hated the zoo; they thought the animals looked so sad in their cages. They found the dinosaur bones in the museum intriguing but were positive that their own private bone collection they had accumulated over the summer from roadkill and predators would be just as impressive if I would only buy them the proper glue so they could put it all together. The Lion House was our last stop. I wanted them to see the charming artistic decorating, the prim and proper straight-backed furniture and the printed carpets. A superbly coiffed matron greeted us at the door for our tour. She looked my children over and then surveyed me, and I thought I sensed just a bit of hesitation in her demeanor. As we walked from room to room through the lovely pioneer home, I became more and more self-conscious. Whenever she turned her back for a moment, I found myself patting loose hairs into place, whispering a reminder to a child to stand up straight, or re-tucking in a shirt. The children were listening intently as our hostess described what life was like in the mid-1800s. She was emphasizing the differences that modern appliances had made in the ease of our everyday living. I could see the wheels turning in my children's little heads. I could see them comparing their current circumstances with what this lady thought only happened in the past. And, the conclusion was dawning on each cherubic face. They were going to tell! My children were going to tell this woman that they knew *exactly* what it was like! Horror was dawning on my face. They would tell all, and Child Services would be sent to come and take my children away. I began to panic and planned our escape as I watched the woman's lips form the question,

"Can you imagine living without hot running water or a toilet in your home?"

I saw four little mouths drop open ready to reply. I clapped my hand over the mouth of the eldest and herded them all right out the door and into the Studebaker which couldn't get us back to Idaho quickly enough. My husband had a good laugh about my fears as I related the story.

"You've done a great job caring for and educating the children," he said. "You don't need to worry about Child Services. No one is going to know or care or question the life we have led this summer."

I was still uneasy about it the next day when I took our son into the elementary school for his kindergarten readiness test. He only missed one question. The teacher had asked him,

"Where do you hang your coat?"

He wrinkled up his brow in perplexed concentration. His teacher waited for a normal response. It wasn't delivered. Instead, he bit his lip and looked up, thinking some more and then finally said,

"On a nail?"

Chimney Fishing in the Rockies

Steve Odenthal

It was just a weekend project. The assignment was nothing too difficult, or at least that's what my wife would later claim. I, of course, knew better. As a permanently scarred veteran of many a weekend project gone awry, I can assure you that any undertaking in the realm of home improvement can be made difficult provided you put the right man on the job. I can also affirm that; indeed, I am that man.

This particular assignment was not delivered via some self-destructing tape, ala Mission Impossible, but rather by my wife, a dangerous and explosive device in her own right. Don't get me wrong; my wife is normally a very mild-mannered individual. She is not given to flights of temper or fantasy, unless, of course, pushed to the breaking point by pure frustration or overwhelming ineptitude. Luckily for her, she gets to hang out with me.

Given her natural bent toward sanity, I was at a complete loss to understand how she had selected me to purchase and install a new fireplace insert. It simply defied all logic given my history of DIY mishaps. I still do believe that she had the very best of intentions and wasn't purposely punishing me. I could be wrong. Perhaps you should be the judge.

✳✳✳

In my wife's mind, a fireplace insert would have been just the thing to give our living room a nice and cozy "kick your shoes off and get comfy" touch. That was certainly the feeling we were going for. That was the game plan. As it was, our existing fireplace had a little different aura to it, more of an "early coal mine–roast a marshmallow and die" kind of thing. Not one of your more desirable auras, true, but one in which we had invested considerable time and many a presto log.

I didn't think there was a great need for a change, but once again, I had been out voted in our little family council. The wife and kids had sided together on this one. It seems they got a little spooked by our last Christmas blaze. The traditional roasting of chestnuts over an open fire got a bit out of control last year. Sure, we lost the stockings, a few presents, the tree and most of the draperies, but there was no real structural damage.

I thought that my wife was over-reacting, but I do love her dearly. She is a wonderful, intelligent, and beautiful woman. Forget the "Lady in Red" we've all heard immortalized in song. That woman can't hold a candle to my wife. No one can, or should, for that matter. You see, she gets pretty nervous around open flames since what we now laughingly refer to as the *Chestnut Incident*. Now, at least, I'm able to laugh about that particular episode. Who knew that overheated chestnuts would become a popcorn monsoon of flaming projectiles? Those fiery nuggets aren't in the song at all! And how was I supposed to know that Uncle Phillip's special eggnog would serve as an accelerant in the blaze? I guess now we know why Uncle Phil is always so jolly around the holidays. As I say, there was no real harm done, and his eyebrows have mostly grown back.

Nevertheless, the die was cast, and I had an official weekend project. Now, for the edification of those of you who have never successfully installed a fireplace insert, and there are many of us out there who still haven't, allow me to elaborate on the steps necessary. It should be a simple four-step process:

First: Purchase (at a reasonable price) a Fireplace Insert.

Second: Prepare the Chimney and Fireplace.

Third: Install the Fireplace Insert.

Fourth: Clean up after the Installation, Firemen, and Paramedics.

The first step would seem to be easy enough to complete. So, *you* say! You might think that competitively shopping the various retailers would produce a list of descending prices, with each store trying to underbid the other hoping to make that sale. Unfortunately, I live in a small town where my reputation as a "do-it-yourselfer" precedes me. Once the word was on the street that I was shopping for a fireplace insert AND intended to do the installation myself, why, prices began to rise. There seemed to be a prevailing fear throughout the retail community that after the general public witnessed the final results of my handiwork, or read the accompanying headlines in the local newspaper, hard-earned business reputations and entire product lines would be in jeopardy. Imagine that!

I was finally able to secure a product that would fit my requirement at a bargain price of 20% over retail. I was amazed at my good fortune. For most of my projects, the standard markup in town was an additional

35%. Of course, there were some conditions. I did have to agree to leave the store empty-handed and wait until midnight for delivery via an unmarked van. Also, all identifying marks and product labels would be filed off of the unit itself to protect the good name of the manufacturer. Step two of my four-pronged attack on lifestyle upgrades proved to be the hardest, at least for my marriage.

Since my wife had conceived this project in the first place, I felt it only proper that she assist in the cleanup and preparation of the fireplace before the actual work began. I'm willing to admit now; that was a mistake. In my defense, I had no way to predict the crude and crusty language that would become so commonplace around our home as the work progressed. And I certainly had no inclination that my father-in-law, yes, her very own father, would have developed such an extensive and salty vocabulary. Not to excuse his actions, rather as a means of introduction, you must know that my father-in-law, Newbie Jenkins, is a man's man, with a workshop to match. There isn't a tool that he hasn't used or made. That works out quite well since there hasn't been a single one of his tools that I haven't had occasion to use and somehow break. Mr. J has always been willing to contribute to my handyman projects — after he's had a chance to survey the damage and, of course, once his laughter had subsided. For this project, I decided to involve him right at the get-go, calling upon his expertise at the very beginning of the prep work. And from all I could ascertain, he was eager to help, although he certainly didn't express that eagerness in words that an untrained ear would pick up on. Around me, he spoke in a special code that the two of us had worked out over the years: I call him Sir or Mr. J, and he would select from his extensive repertoire an ever-changing assortment of endearing names for me. We began work in earnest on a fine Saturday morning.

I had slept in that morning, as the midnight delivery previously arraigned for had occurred closer to 2:30 AM and involved not only an unmarked van but also several unmarked police cars and a chauffeured trip downtown before all the confusion was straightened out. It can be a lengthy discussion explaining the lack of identifying markings and serial numbers on a delivery van and its contents to law enforcement officials at that time of day. Exhausted and with nerves a bit frayed, I had prepared for bed and then decided to soothe myself before actually retiring with a nice cup of hot chocolate while stretching out in my favorite leather recliner in the front room. Things already seemed better, and I relaxed for what must have been just a few minutes before I was awakened by the gentle rap of Mr. J's monkey wrench upon the double-pane window directly above my head. Luckily, it was only the outer pane that shattered and the sudden adrenal rush that it gave me eliminated any need for my

7 AM exercise regimen. I immediately met and surpassed my target aerobic heart rate. I was up and out the door in a flash as apparently time was a-wasting.

Mr. J was already propping a ladder against the house. Trying hard to be of immediate use and match the energy of my father-in-law, I scrambled up that ladder and onto the roof. Hands-on-hips and steely-eyed, I surveyed the situation. Standing there, atop my version of a *man's castle*, I breathed in the crisp morning air and cast a watchful eye over the surrounding neighborhood. My gaze fell upon fellow handymen about to tackle their honey-do lists. They seemed to regard me with a certain amount of awe, pointing and waving, smiling and laughing and I knew at once that I had been adopted into the swelling ranks of local weekend Bob the Builders. I was sure that if I yelled out, "Can We Fix It?" I would hear echoing back from my fellow Bobs a resounding "Yes We Can!"

Proudly, I looked below to where my father-in-law was leaning against his truck, working his cuticles with a buck knife. "What ya doin' up there?" he asked.

"I'm ready to start," I replied.

"Really? I kinda figured you'd probably want your tool belt," he said.

My hands dropped to my waist and groped feverishly. Nothing. Embarrassed, I scrambled back down the ladder. As I passed the old comedian, heading into the house to retrieve my tool belt, he chuckled,

"While you're in there, Junior, you might consider putting some britches on… although those long-johns are downright stylish."

My father-in-law has never been mistaken for Mr. Blackwell, so I had a pretty good idea that he was being sarcastic. As I retreated into the house, I considered his comment as well as a half a dozen responses that I might have used to counter his fashion critique, but ultimately thought the better of them and returned to the work area more adequately attired for the job ahead. I stepped outside just in time to catch a small, leashed porcupine that had somehow discovered the wonders of flight and was flying rapidly towards me.

"Think fast!" yelled Mr. J.

"Ow!" was my response as I caught not a porcupine, but a steel-wired chimney brush with not a leash but a rope attached.

"Where're your gloves? Can't work without gloves. Especially up there cleaning the chimney. You'll have to use the rope; I lost the extension poles."

"Ow!" again was my reply, as I still was in pain. "What if that was not me but your daughter coming out the door?"

"*She'd* have been wearing gloves—there's work to do. Stop your bleeding, and let's get started. I'm gonna go check the damper." And with that, Mr. J disappeared into the house.

I carefully pulled the steel wires that had broken skin from one palm and then the other, a process that freed me from the chimney brush, and provided me a memory which I have no wish to ever re-live. My wife appeared at the door with some soothing ointment and bandages on cue—being the true angel of mercy that she is. As she gently attended to my hands, I mentioned that I was glad at least her father had sent her out to treat me.

She nodded and said: "He didn't. I was setting up the nurses' station like I always do when you have a DIY weekend. When you work with Dad, you *always* wear gloves!" she replied as she finished her Florence Nightingale duties and handed me a pair.

"A helmet and bike leathers might be smart too," I mumbled as I slid on the gloves and ascended the ladder with my porcupine in tow. I was eager to show Mr. J that this project was still under control and that he and I could work as a solid team. I approached the chimney with caution and peered down into its dark abyss.

It was a quiet kind of darkness down there, at first, but then I thought I heard a slight scratching noise. I moved in closer, bringing my head so close to the opening that all light was blocked. Still, more scratching. The closer I put my head into the brick cylinder, the more definite and intense the scratching became, then it struck me, Mr. J was inside fiddling with the damper. Of course. I should let him know I was ready for action up top. So, I called out to him.

"Mr. J—I'm ready to—"

Squirrels can jump *really* high and scamper *really*, *really* fast. Especially when experiencing what they could only equate as a total eclipse of the sun. Some moon-sized object had obliterated all of the light in their world—and then started speaking to them in tongues they knew little of. In retrospect, I can now see their plight and why they took to their heels. As I staggered back out of their path, I wished that I had worn those leathers and helmet. That little bit of extra attire might have slowed the rascals down as they scampered and leaped to the safety of the nearest oak tree. The helmet might have saved the indignity of their loss of traction on my already thinning hair. It would take quite a while before those scratches would heal and I could return to my regular use of Vitalis—a popular and alcohol-based hair tonic of the day.

"You're up there playing with your hair? Sheesh. Well, when you're all done spritzin' up, we've got a job to do." Mr. J was on the lawn again. "Something's jammed in the damper. Probably the remains of that chestnut meat you treated us to at Christmas. See if you can help me get it open. Wedge the brush against the damper—don't scratch it against the sides on the way down now. Make sure you don't. Just lower it down the center. Nice and easy. After I get the damper open, I'll reach up and clear out some of that Christmas junk by hand. Then we'll spread all the sheets, and you can do all the scraping you want when we have everything all covered up down here. Don't want to make a mess in my own daughter's house."

And then he was gone, back inside the house. I didn't think I was supposed to salute, but son-in-lawin' was still a new thing to me. His plan sounded like it would work to me, and I tried my very best to comply. Holding the rope tightly over the chimney opening, I began to lower my friend the porcupine down into the chasm of chestnut-goodness, and somehow, it found the damper on the very first plunge. Although I could not see the bottom, I knew the sound immediately as the metallic brush landed on top of the damper, which was ajar enough for Mr. J to have worked his fingers through. That also meant that there was enough room for the chimney brush to work its spiny bristles into the opening as well.

Further confirmation of the brush's arrival was obtained in the guttural howl that Mr. J let loose as ol' Porky unleashed at least one quill into his probing fingers.

"Mr. J! Are you not wearing gloves?" I couldn't resist as I pulled up sharply on the rope to open the damper.

"Mphmmack…" or words to that effect was the retort I heard between the coughing and gasping down below. Not the "job well done" I had been expecting. I looked back down the chimney and beheld a very well-sooted and angry man. And as I tried to see past those anger-tinged eyeballs, I could see that the fireplace, hearth, and no doubt the room that stretched out below had taken on the singed and sooty chestnut haze of last Christmas. It was also very evident to me that I wouldn't hear "Ho Ho Ho" or the singing of carols anytime soon.

"I thought I told you, NO SCRATCHING! NO SCRATCHING!"

"I didn't scratch–I promise!" I yelled back down the chimney. And then it came to me—the squirrels! Apparently, when a herd of those rascals stampede, their scampering squirrel hoofs will pull everything loose as they attempt to gain upward trajectory. I put forth my theory:

"It, it was a herd of squirrels. I swear. I didn't scratch. Really! It was them." And for effect, I pointed accusingly at the neighboring oak trees.

There were doubters. Mr. J's voice boomed, "Squirrels? There was a herd of—in the chimney? Only you saw them. That… That's your story?"

He had come back out to the lawn now and was looking directly at me with eyes that seemed a little less threatening and a bit more comical. He looked like someone had applied mascara with a blow-dryer. I didn't trust those raccoon-ish eyes. I clung to the safety of the chimney. I was nodding vigorously and pantomiming the furry chestnut-lovers escape route, hoping to add credibility to my affirmation.

"Squirrels… a whole pack of them. Yes, Sir."

Time slipped away quietly as I stood frozen on the roof, and Mr. J took a slow and silent inventory of where exactly common sense might have leaked from my body. After a few moments, he gave up on his quest. His body sagged back into that half-dejected, half-amused posture he leaned into when both I and his truck were in his proximity. Shaking his head in quiet amusement, he repeated,

"Squirrels, huh?" Then Mr. J gestured with his palms up in surrender, "Well, you never know? You never know."

He slid into the driver's seat and started the engine. "Got the shop-vac fixed again—you're gonna need it in there. No wet cement this time, alright?" he grinned. "And make sure you bring my chimney brush back too." Mr. J gunned the engine, gave a wave and then the suddenly happy raccoon, done for the day, motored off in search of a much safer, and cleaner place.

At this point, I had a choice to make. Was I going to do the right thing and survey the damage inside our home? That *would* be the appropriate thing to do. Or was I going to finish my job on the roof and face the music *after* I had completed the chimney cleaning chore I had started? My wife was in the house, not on the roof, so it was a rather easy choice. I climbed the ladder.

Walking up the shingled incline to the chimney, I was surprised to see that the herd of squirrels had returned to the scene of their crime. I approached the brick and mortar with caution as there were quite a number of the hooligans assembled, and they collectively had a look in their eyes that made them a mob. Had they been holding pitchforks and torches; I would not have been surprised. The majority of the little beasties gave ground and defiantly scattered (which is much more desirable than their stampede method of departing), while I could see a few other furry little protesters clinging onto ol' Porky's rope as it dangled from the chimney.

In my haste, I did not think to find a helmet before climbing back onto the shingled battlefield, so I was understandably somewhat cautious as I shooed the little rascals away. Once the last feisty nut-muncher had leaped to the safety of a nearby tree, I began the process of retrieving my buddy the porcupine by pulling the rope up and out of the chimney.

It was going to be a chore, but somehow, I was determined to make Newbie's free-range chimney brush just the right tool to clean this bad boy. I pulled on the slack of the rope only to find that there was no slack. Ol' Porky must be still caught on the damper, I reasoned. Well, maybe a big tug on the rope would set it free. I gave my best effort at a tug, and the rope instantly came free. The rope came up so easily; I was amazed and watched it arch and shift in the air above me. I was so intrigued by the design that loose rope made during its flight that, at first, I didn't notice that there were still a couple of very surprised long-tails doing their best to walk an ever-changing tight-rope mid-air. Once I did realize that Chip and Dale's cousins were scampering down the rope, which now floated above my head, with an angry look in their eye, it was too late for me to take any evasive or protective action. All I could do was cringe and tighten my body into a stone-like statue while I endured being the last hop to freedom for these final two chimney protectors.

Although not as painful as the full stampede earlier had been, the experience was not one I would recommend anyone trying at home. The rope fell limply at my feet. After carefully verifying there were no more chimney dwellers lurking, I examined the rope. I had one end in my hand, and as I stooped to pick up the other end, I could not help but notice that my porcupine, Newbie's favorite chimney brush, was nowhere to be found. Where ol' Porky should have been there was just a well-gnawed piece of rope. Realizing that this could only mean that my borrowed porcupine was still at the bottom of the chimney, I shook my fist in the direction of the squirrel-laden trees and cried out unto that wilderness, giving full voice to my frustration.

Midway through my epitaph, which I thought was one for the ages, my wife appeared on the lawn below.

"You're yelling at the squirrels?" She had a point.

I stopped and sheepishly protested, "They started it…"

"The neighbors," she said as she gestured toward the street.

I knew she was right; I must have looked quite silly up there carrying on like that. I looked around at the surrounding yards and without exception, all the Bobs, who I had on my team earlier this morning, had stopped their chores and were staring quietly up at me. Some were even shaking their heads just a little. Embarrassed, I looked back down at my wife, still a lovely vision despite being lightly dusted with soot. She even made that look work—not like her dad, who just wasn't able to pull off any look involving eyeliner. Her disappointed gaze didn't help me stand any taller, and I was only able to offer a feeble defense of my outburst.

"Squirrels…", I mumbled. One of my elderly neighbors sidled up to her and said while pointing at me on the roof.

"He's acting pretty silly up there making all that racket, Valerie. Is he on some medications? Gonna bring property values down. We want a nice quiet neighborhood, you know. Don't let him do the handyman thing. What is it this time?"

"Hello, Robert. Sorry about the noise but he's done yelling at *anything* now." She made sure I understood her emphasis.

I shook my fist one last time in the direction of the furry marauders.

"I hope so. It's a quiet neighborhood. We like that. Saw the cop cars last night and I knew he was at it again. Did you let him watch another Bob Villa TV show, or what?"

"No," Val kindly said as she led Robert into our home. "Let me show you what we are up to."

I was glad to have them gone. Robert was an antique version of my father-in-law, and as such, he needed to be handled carefully. He had ended his official Bob the Builder phase years ago and had entered into a "lean on a shovel and opine advice to whippersnappers" stanza of life. I needed to think about the dilemma I now faced. I still had a chimney to clean. Newbie was looking forward to a reunion at some time with his favorite brush which now lay helpless somewhere at the bottom of the dark and dirty bricked shaft. I did have the rope which originally might have helped in the cleaning as it was then attached to the brush, but in its present state, any magical scrubbing powers it might have had vanished with its disassociation from ol' Porky.

Additionally, I could hear the murmuring of the motley crew reassembling in the trees, plotting a new assault to win their Chimney of Chestnutty Goodness. Those ruffians hoped to make it their own once more. My task was going to take some figuring all right. I pulled my trusty flashlight from my toolbelt and looked into the chimney stack. There it was. My spiny friend, the chimney brush, lay motionless on top of the damper beyond my reach. Perhaps I could snare it with the rope, I thought. I quickly tied a slip knot on one end and lowered it into the dark cavern. It took some doing, but I managed to work the opening over the bristles and lift the brush up into the air just a bit. This attack was working! In my excitement and haste to rescue the untethered ball of scratches, I had failed to synch up the slip knot, and four bricks from my reach, the metallic quill pig escaped its noose and dove back into the shaft.

I shined the beam of light back down and realized that my elusive friend was now standing on his head, jammed between the damper assembly and the bricked side of the chimney. It would be senseless to attempt the rope trick to retrieve it from its deeply wedged position. Anyone could see that. It would be a complete waste of time. That is, however, one thing that I am good at, completely wasting time, and so I pursued that course of folly for another forty-five minutes before coming up with another can't miss strategy.

I needed a magnet. Not a small one, either—no refrigerator magnet would do this job. It struck me that my father-in-law had just the thing. I had to get the shop-vac anyway; if I was sneaky, I could borrow his prized, treasure-hunting magnet at the same time. This was a magnet that made refrigerator magnets cringe in fear of a fatal attraction.

Ol' Buford, as Newbie liked to call his prize, could remove fillings from teeth at twenty paces. It was big; weighed about thirty pounds and was circular in design. Picture a kind of a home version of the magnets you see lifting cars in a junkyard. I would spare Newbie the details of exactly *why* I needed his iron pride and joy, but once back I would attach it to the rope and make quick work of the retrieval of ol' Porky.

I quickly descended the ladder and rushed into the house which now had the pleasant smell of melted Chestnuts and the hint of a Christmas fog in the air. Valerie and Robert stood a bit further into the room, surveying the damage. Robert unfolded his arms and glanced at me with those wide eyes of his. His glances always either portrayed astonishment or revealed a madman when we got together for any length of time.

"I'm going to run and get the shop-vac from your Dad."

"That will help, dear. How is it going up there, anyway?"

"Just about got it." I lied and beat a hasty retreat before any further questioning took place.

Once at my in-laws' home, I headed straight for the tool shed. If I played this right, I could be in and out and avoid all human contact. I swung the door open and was face to face with Mr. J. He hadn't washed his face yet, and he was practicing with a fly rod in the suddenly small enclosure.

"Watch yourself, Junior." He cautioned as a fly darted in my direction about eye-level. I ducked and bobbed to the left as the danger end whipped past me on the right, snagging and tearing my baseball cap off en route to the far end of the lawn.

"That out there…That's the deep end." Newby seemed satisfied with his cast, and as he reeled my hat back in, he continued. "I suppose you are here to get the shop-vac. Like my new rod?"

He did not give me a chance to respond. "Why don't you take my old one over there? I'll teach you how to use it sometime. Don't mind the duct tape and gorilla glue; she's still as strong as the day I found her. Sorta."

With that, he pulled ol' Snappy, formerly his favorite fly-fishing rod from its pegboard mount, presented it to me and without too much ceremony placed his new prize rod on the pegboard place of honor.

"I kept the reel seat and fly line but the fighting butt, that's yours. Remember to shut off the light when you go."

Whistling a song that somehow reminded me of an Old Spice commercial, the raccoon-eyed angler departed for the house. Sometimes Mr. J spoke in tongues around me, and at that moment, I wasn't exactly sure *why* he had called me a "fighting butt," but I chose to take it as a compliment. Later I would understand that it was the name of a part of my new rod, ol' Snappy.

As soon as he was out of sight, I grabbed the shop-vac and wrestled it open. The metallic base was empty, and shiny clean as Mr. J's tools always are. I rolled the vac out and around to the back of the shed. Now would be my chance to grab ol' Buford and hide it away in the shop vac's base. If all went well, Mr. J would never know that Buford had strayed.

Because of its tremendous power, the big magnet had to live a life of isolation high on a wooden shelf next to the back door of the shed. Buford had proved early on that he needed to be by an exit for safety reasons. The story I had heard was that when Mr. J first tried to bring the great magnet into the shed, he opened the door and was immediately set upon by all manner of Craftsman hand tools from the pegboard and various shelves. Most of the proclaimed witnesses say that they have never seen Newbie move so fast, jump so high, or dance so comically. Of course, most of those storytellers don't make mention of the incident when Mr. J is in the same room.

I took the big magnet from its shelf and deposited it as quietly as I could into the barrel of the shop-vac, then replaced the top. *So far, so good.* I started back up the cement toward my truck with my new rod, and the shop-vac with its assorted tools and hoses in tow. I had parked behind Mr. J's truck, and we had almost reached his vehicle when I felt ol' Buford kicking in. The shop-vac rushed on ahead to greet the front bumper of Newbie's prized pickup. As the two collided, I felt a presence by my side.

"What the—Why'd you throw the shop-vac at my truck? Here. Let me get it."

Newbie lifted the shop-vac into his arms and struggled his way around his truck unknowingly having to use his body to minimize ol' Bufford's magnetic strength.

"This shop-vac, ugh, sure don't seem to want to go with you. Maybe I didn't get all the cement out of it. Treat it nice this time."

Mr. J lifted the vacuum into the bed of my truck and watched, amazed as it immediately scooted to the nearest corner and hugged both the tailgate and sidewall. Having still not washed his face, Mr. J looked like a very puzzled burglar.

"I think the poor thing is afraid of you. It's cringin' in the corner. Incredible!"

After he walked away, shaking his head, I jumped back into the cab and made my way back to our humble abode. Arriving there safely, which is unusual, I couldn't help but notice that ol' Robert had rustled up a few of the neighborhood Bobs and had them clustered in a huddle on the lawn. Apparently, he was about to call a play. Not on my watch! I jumped from the vehicle before the lead Bob could reach me and spun back to the tailgate.

I quickly popped the head off of the shop-vac as it sat trembling in the corner of the bed and grabbed ol' Buford the magnet. Holding the iron circle of attraction on my outside hip with my left hand, I staggered past my truck and headed straight for the ladder.

Lead Bob sang out, "Need a hand?" and probably meant it, but I was too busy implementing my plan.

"No thanks, I've got this,"

I grunted as I moved toward the ladder. I was hoping to get a running start and get onto the roof as quickly as possible, thus limiting the time exposed to Robert and his gang of kibitzers. I knew what I was doing. My right hand gripped the side of the ladder, and I took the first three rungs with ease. Rungs four and five were a bit of a strain as ol' Buford in my left hand had smelled the metal of the ladder, and my ascent began to skew to the left. With only three steps to go Buford got the better of me and clanged into the metal side of Mr. J's non-aluminum (of course) ladder. My tug of war with ol' Buford was a mismatch, and I quickly found myself dangling from the old iron ring between the ladder and the house. Not for long, though as I then felt myself slipping down the rail with the magnet as it made its way to the ground. Then, it was all kinds of dark.

I wasn't badly damaged, and as I blinked my vision back into place, I saw Robert standing above me attempting to light the fire in the bowl of his pipe. A few of his assembled Bobs circled as well. As Robert's cheeks sucked in and out and his flame danced you could tell he was formulating a decree of some kind. He took a deep draw on his pipe of wisdom and pointed a bony finger at me.

"No more Bob Villa for you. No more!"

The brotherhood of Bobs around me mumbled their agreement. The old wizard continued,

"I had the boys tie your magnet to the rope," he gestured toward the roof. "It's up there by the chimney. Yes. I know about the brush. You'll have to fish for it. Satisfy an old man's curiosity. Why weren't you using the poles that come with it?"

I was pretty much recovered and thinking straight now. I wasn't sure he deserved an answer, but I gave him one anyway.

"Mr. J—repurposed them—somewhere. They weren't in the kit when he loaned it to me."

"Sounds like ol' Newbie," the old expert laughed between puffs of smoke. "Well you've still got his rope, but you better retrieve that brush. Jenkins men are pretty attached to their tools."

"Don't I know that," I mumbled and maneuvered to the ladder again. "How long was I out?" I asked, rubbing my head where apparently ol' Buford, the ground, and my head had made contact.

"Not long. A little nap," the pipe of wisdom offered.

I ascended the ladder to what had been my domain, my outpost, my safe place (despite the squirrels). A place where once I believed I was in control of this project and my fate. That seemed so long ago, now. I looked over to the chimney. The Bobs, no doubt under the direction of ol' Robert, had indeed fastened Buford to the rope and in a nice touch also had included ol' Snappy, my new fly rod in the mix. They had also set up a lawn chair as they anticipated landing this catch would not be quick.

I could not help but laugh as I looked back down onto the lawn and beheld the smiles of the many Bobs and their assorted Bobettes below.

"Sandwiches!" I heard my lovely wife cry as she brought a serving board full of lunch to the famished crowd below. Quickly the small crowd organized itself into neat arrays of picnic benches and tables from the various backyards represented. Somehow this had become a block party with noise and merriment all around.

"I'll be right down. I could go for a sandwich." I started toward the ladder just as my lovely wife popped her head up over the rooftop.

She was bringing my lunch to me. A paper plate of sandwiches and her smile never looked so good. I gladly took them and set the plate atop the chimney for safekeeping.

"Not so fast. You get to stay here," she said as she stepped off the ladder and onto the roof. "Now, I know this was your project, and, well, it got off to a bit of a rocky start with my Dad this morning. So, while you were gone, Robert organized some things and some of the neighbors—and, well—WE'RE DONE! it's all set!"

I chuckled. "But the room? And I still have to clean the chimney…"

"Done and Done. Phil had a complete chimney brush kit. He finished in no time. And Robert grabbed his shop-vac."

"Phil?"

"Phil Epstein. Phil and Janice? Two houses down?"

"Phil? Oh, you mean, *Lead Bob*, right. Well, good ol' Robert. That was nice of him—and them… after lunch, I'll get right on the actual install…"

"Done."

"What?"

She sounded apologetic as she said, "We started to get such a big group here, and they all wanted to help. They *really* did do a nice job."

"So, what you're saying is, the project is done?"

"Mostly—"

"What's left. I can do it!"

"I know that you can. And everyone is counting on you! Take your time with that magnet, and I am sure that you can retrieve Dad's chimney brush before you know it."

"It won't take long," I said quite confidently. "If somebody wants pictures, they better snap fast."

"Oh, that's a great idea. I hadn't thought of that!"

She descended the ladder to join the jovial picnickers. Sighing, I reached over to my plate and came up empty. I turned just in time to see five squirrels and my sandwich leaping to the neighbor's tree. Each half of the sandwich was astride a pair of escaping fur-frogs and, I swear I saw the fifth squirrel turn back and shake his fist at me. In a bit of cosmic comeuppance my empty plate, aided by a quick gust of wind, slapped me in the face as the furry commandos beat their hasty retreat.

Somewhat dejected now and feeling older than my years, I pulled the lawn chair closer, picked up ol' Snappy and half-heartedly cast ol' Buford down into the abyss. I hit immediately; I heard the contact as the magnet found the damper, and my rope line went taut. There would be no great battle–I knew when I was beaten—bested by ol' Buford. I wasn't the first, but I might be the last to make such a claim. The great magnet was never letting go. Buford knew it. I knew it. Heck, even the snickering squirrels in the trees knew it. All that was left was to await the paparazzi below to embrace this photo-op. And they did. Various images of me in my lawn chair engaged in catch and release, against the backdrop of the mighty Rocky Mountains became a local favorite. For several years, I was asked to reprise the pose for photojournalists who wrote either inspiring stories of hope or studies on early dementia. I accommodated them all.

✳✳✳

About once a year, I still climb the ladder and visit ol' Porky and Buford. They remain, silent guardians of our chimney damper and I like to think objects of mystic worship for the bravest among our neighborhood squirrel population. Eventually, and in my own way, I did let Mr. J know about his brush and his prized magnet. He handled the news and the messenger in a uniquely Newbie Jenkins way—but that is another story for another time.

When the Going Gets Tough There Is Always the Window

Steve Odenthal

My neighbor's teenaged son, we'll call him Brenton to disguise his identity, experienced his very first date a few weeks ago. The day and evening turned out to be a resounding and innocent success enjoyed by all. But like all first dates, this evening wasn't without moments of trepidation for my young friend. Moments of trepidation always intrigue me and are always a good indicator of a Chimney Fishing story worth sharing. Luckily, Brenton, without too much arm-twisting, confided his adventure in me, and I am sure he wouldn't mind my sharing it with you. Pretty sure.

Doing the sensible thing for a novice, our young hero arranged for a couple of his buddies to make this a group date, where all the young couples knew each other and felt, if not comfortable, at least some degree of calmness in a potentially stressful circumstance. On the appointed day Brenton joined up with his friends as they picked up their dates and headed off to a day of no-pressure fun before the school dance.

Each of the group gathered were approximately equally experienced with the whole boy/girl thing, and they immediately felt comfortable with one another. The day had been carefully planned out and scheduled, mainly by the young ladies in the group, with the idea of keeping the herd moving and having fun. Stops were to occur along the way at the girls' homes where each young lady, in turn, served as a hostess for some unique activity that she or her family would sponsor. Depending upon the interests of the individual families involved, the activities seemed to vary greatly—some presenting a physical challenge, others offering a mental test of sorts—the trick seemed to be avoiding awkwardness. That, of course, should be no problem for teenaged boys, right?

As the day progressed, Brenton and his date had a most enjoyable time mixing with various and sundry friends, family members and an occasional wandering stranger who was inadvertently sucked into the group's vortex as it spun hectically through our small town. With each home visited the young men and women seemed more and more relaxed with one another. The only one who seemed at all tense was an occasional father who realized that his teenaged daughter had ignored sage advice and decided to date before age thirty-one. But I'm sure they will get over it.

All systems were go for Brenton right up until the time the group arrived at the home of the special girl who was his date. (We'll call her Hannah in this story.) Then inexplicably, our hero felt just a little bit of hesitancy in his step as Hannah grabbed his hand and began pulling him toward the backyard of her home, leading the group to where the fun was scheduled to continue. Brenton had never met the family but had heard a few things around town about her father and knew him by sight—a bear of a man. Hesitancy was contagious that day as Brenton noticed that the other boys had adopted his slow pace.

The girls were laughing and chattering away without a care as they each pulled their particular boy back to an area of the yard where a ten-foot table sat arrayed with an arsenal of highly polished, stainless-steel hatchets. Behind the table, dressed in buckskin and fringe, sat Hannah's family, smiling broadly. It was obvious that the small tribe had been waiting for their daughter's group and by their body language seemed quite anxious to get the backyard festivities underway. Hannah's father turned off the welcoming glow of his massive smile and rose from his seat. Just when he seemed to block out the sun, it seemed to Brenton that he kept on rising even higher above the boys. He moved to the group of boys and inspected the troops.

"Which one of you young men are accompanying my daughter today?" His tone was calm and controlled; however, his un-squinted eye captured an inner beast.

"That would be me, Sir," Brenton answered, and his hands began to sweat just a little.

The father stopped and pivoted back to face him. "You. You're the lucky one, are you?" His voice, as Brenton tells it, was not so menacing as much as his demeanor moving in close and asking the question two inches from his face.

"Yes, sir. I guess I am. I guess—"

"Well, then. It's your honor…" The father said with an eerie half-smile while picking up a hatchet from the table and sliding his fingers lightly across the sharp blade.

"S—s—sir?"

"To throw, Son. To throw!" The mountain-man thrust the hatchet into Brenton's hand while grabbing the boy's shoulders, turning him toward the house thirty feet away. An old archery target and stand stood on the shadowy crest of the rising knoll upon which the family home sat.

"Mind, there's not much of a wind today, but you *will* have to compensate for the elevation. Use your full arm, boy, or you'll never make it to the target." Brenton was apprehensive, and a bit unnerved at having to go first. Sensing that, the father nudged him to the side and said, "Watch this. It's easy."

With that, the older man flung his sharp object casually. The hatchet landed directly in the center of the target with a thud.

"Nothing to it. Your turn."

Suddenly, Brenton realized that his friends were offering him moral support by agreeing. "Nothing to it!" "You've got this." were among the platitudes that rang out from the others, his buddies who secretly were so grateful they did not have to lead off in this game. Their encouragement seemed to help, and he felt his hands go from sweaty to just clammy.

As he took his stance and his arm went into throwing motion, Brenton felt in control–right up til the release part. It was then that he realized that he had misjudged a bit, and in reality, his hand was still sweaty. The hatchet took flight. While the weapon flew, his buddies were complimentary of his throwing motion and form. Some of the girls started to clap. Too soon, *way too soon.*

For that brief moment of flight, it seemed that only Brenton and Hannah's father could appreciate what was coming. A gasp escaped Brenton's lips, while a lower guttural groan issued from the father's throat. And then—the crash of glass was heard as the hatchet found itself in the bedroom on the right of the target, no doubt embedded in the wall or perhaps a Barbie playhouse. Dead silence fell upon the group of happy youth, mid-cheer.

"My window!" came the small voice of Hannah's younger sister behind the table.

"What the—Heck!" As well as a few other special remarks flowed forth from the father's general vicinity as he came to grips with the situation.

"I told you we should have just played Parcheesi, Lowell!" Hannah's mother spoke for the very first time.

"How was I supposed to know he couldn't throw?" His date's father asked pretty much anyone at the scene.

"Lowell don't be mean. I'm sure he's sorry. Not everyone can throw a weapon." Mother was trying to help.

"I think I'm done." Brenton retreated.

"No. No, you're not. When you fall off a horse you've got to get right back on," Lowell explained as he handed Brenton another hatchet and patted him on the back. "Make your peace with it, Son. Maybe aim a bit to the left this time, just a little."

The frontiersman's voice seemed controlled, and his words rang with true encouragement to Brenton's ears, but something about the renewed squint and rapid eye movement gave him pause. Not to mention Jim Bridger's rapid breathing and the two-inch, Drill Sergeant closeness sent a mixed message. Brenton looked over at his buddies and their dates. Not a lot of encouragement from over there. He looked toward his date, Hannah, but she looked a bit dazed and confused. A couple of nervous laughs scattered around the backyard, but in truth, they may have been emitted by the neighbors who by now had gathered at the fence line. Otherwise, not much sound came forth. It was pretty quiet.

This time as he took the hatchet, Brenton rubbed his throwing hand on his pant leg, making sure his grip was dry.

"Are you sure you want me to throw again?"

"Absolutely." Lowell made sure his eye contact was solid and noticeably wild. "Remember, be strong and follow through. Do it, Son."

Bolstered by the half-crazed father figure, Brenton took his stance again and inhaled deeply.

Exhaling in a steady forced stream, our hero went through the throwing motion and adjusted a bit to the left as he let the hatchet release from his grip. This one was solid and on a perfect line as it approached the standing target—sailing above the mark and to the left, entering the second bedroom window, breaking the glass as the hatchet flew out of sight.

It had been such a perfect day to that point, Poor Brenton, in his dismay, didn't realize that it still was. He had, after all, gone two for two on the day which in baseball would have been lights out. Even if Brenton had put the baseball analogy together at the time, he instinctively knew that there would be no third at-bat. At least, the kitchen window was safe.

As Brenton tells it now, Mrs. Lowell, Hannah's mother, was *reasonably* forgiving of his lack of accuracy. However, she was less than complimentary of her husband's choice of activity for the young teens to enjoy.

Meanwhile, Lowell was speechless and needed to sit down for a while. He did look tired. Hannah rallied and seemed to be quite concerned about Brenton's feelings, realizing that he must feel terrible.

When the understandable chaos calmed a bit, the group decided that it was time to skip ahead to the refreshments. There were, after all, only so many windows on the home. There wouldn't be enough to go around. The couples stood solemnly and drank punch while making small talk about anything except hatchets and windows. Soon it was time to leave for more scheduled frivolity down the road.

As each of the couples made their way toward the assorted vehicles, Brenton heard some muffled laughter and the word *Awesome* here and there. He looked over at the date on his arm and couldn't help but say, "I'm *so* very sorry—" Hannah, being wise beyond her years, calmly replied,

"No. Don't worry. I'm just so glad we didn't have to play Parcheesi!"

✻✻✻

In the time since Brenton confided in me, Lowell has decided to install triple-pane windows throughout the house—a project that Mrs. Lowell has had on the honey-do list for quite a while. Also, you will be glad to hear that young Brenton has made several voyages back out into the turbulent sea of teen dating and seems no worse for it. So, it was as happy an ending, as one could expect for all concerned, I would say.

Now, a word of caution here, Brenton told me this story in the strictest of confidence, so I will trust you not to pass it around. Have we got a deal? Alright, then. He also wondered if his Chimney Fishing moment qualified him as a true Chimney fisherman. You see, being my neighbor, he is well aware that I am a Master-level black belt in the ways of Chimney Fishing.

I was kind. The young man does have a way to go, but I told him he had *definitely* made a start on the path. He has made a start, indeed.

The Last Defiance of a Reluctant Churchgoer

James D Beers

In the beginning, God said, let there be Church. And there was. At least as far as I can remember. That's back four decades, so things are a bit fuzzy, but Church was definitely there in the beginning. As was church going.

As soon as I made my mortal debut, my parents tried to instill in me good church attendance habits. First, they wrapped me tightly in a blanket and carted me around to different church meetings throughout the week (pre-three-hour-block days). Of course, I don't remember any of that, but the subconscious message rang loud and clear—thou shalt go to church.

When I was a baby, Church was pretty easy going— sleep, drink milk, poop. I could've been anywhere for all I knew. But when I started to crawl, Church got boring. I resorted to fidgeting in my parents' arms and then crying when I couldn't crawl under the pews.

Occasionally my parents coaxed me into a nap and nipped my church-going defiance in the bud. Once I started walking, I upped the ante a bit and began escaping pew rows in short sprints. But my parents also improved their game, tricking me into quietly attending church by stuffing me full of snacks. It was devious but effective.

Eventually, however, they had to resort to other covert methods.

"Ooh, do you want to go and play with the toys in the nursery?"

"If you're a good little boy, you can have some Cheerios."

Words like toys and Cheerios worked like magic. They put me under a reverence spell where I forgot about church boredom. By the time I was three, however, I had developed a serious case of independence, and I also figured out what my parents were doing. No longer would I be tricked into going to church quietly.

I tried to warn my younger sister, but the magic powers of toys and Cheerios proved too strong for her to overcome. I'm not sure what happened exactly, but at about the same time I turned three, church boredom increased several-fold. It also turned scary and painful.

Let me explain with a routine church-going scenario. After wrestling kids into church clothes on Sunday mornings, Mom would herd us out to the plastic upholstered Volkswagen Rabbit. If it were winter, Dad would be under the Rabbit's hood trying to lift the little car's spirits with a blow dryer. In summer, he'd have all the doors open trying to fan out the heat with a floor mat.

When Mom had us herded up to the car, she'd open the door and tell us to get inside. We'd stand there staring at either a frozen expanse of hyper-chilled seats of death or a sizzling griddle of molten, butt-blistering plastic. As usual, we'd be late, and Mom wouldn't have time for mild coaxing, so she'd swiftly boot us inside and slam the door before we could escape.

My sister and I would weep and wail and gnash our teeth while we either burned or froze nearly to death in the plastic seats. And that's why I began to associate going to church with pain.

The scary part of Church usually came about fifteen minutes into Sacrament meeting. And I don't mean hellfire and damnation from the pulpit. My legs would start to wiggle, followed by the rest of my body, especially my non-whispering mouth. Cheerios at this point were futile. And toys were handy tools in my noise making. Mom would give me a warning, but thirty seconds later, I'd be at it again. After several threats, my flustered mom would finally turn me over to Dad. Dad would throw me in a full-nelson and drag me out of the chapel quicker than a rattlesnake strike.

For some kids, a trip out of the chapel is a break from church boredom. Not so in my case. I had heard about the devil during Primary class, but I had no idea he could possess my dad. Dad would take me into one of the empty classrooms and hover in front of the door so that I couldn't make a run for it. Then he'd give me a quick swat to the bum followed by his scare-the-hell-out-of-me, forefinger-wagging sermon on being reverent. After that, it was back to the chapel where, thanks to fear and pain, my going-to-church rebellion was significantly quelled.

For some reason, my dad's sermons never stuck, and the Sunday trips to the empty classroom continued. It didn't help that church had gone to the three-hour block schedule and the ensuing boredom threatened to strangle me. On top of that, I had a new baby brother, which contributed to my parents' waning patience for church-going rebellion.

Finally, I decided I would take a stand. So, at the mature age of four, tired of the painful, scary, and boring parts of Church, I told my mom one Sunday morning that I wasn't going to attend church. Her response surprised me. "Okay then, we'll see you when we get home." And just like that, she left with my brother and sister. She must be bluffing, I thought, but a peek out the living-room window revealed the Rabbit making its way out of the driveway.

Frantic, I grabbed my church clothes. My pants in one hand and my shirt in the other, I tore off after my mom sporting only my untied shoes and Superman Underoos. I caught her just before she hit the main road, yanked the door open, and jumped in the car, tears, and whimpers flowing. "I want to go to Church!" I yelled, fully leaving behind my last act of church-going defiance. And that's all it took; that little shock that my mom was actually going to leave me at home. To this day I'm an anxious and willing churchgoer... as long as my wife brings the Cheerios.

About Our Humorists and this Book

Heard at a UTAH Diner is a result of some very good writers taking a chance on an idea. That idea was to highlight a little bit about the state of Utah and its residents using humor. I am so glad that these humorists answered the call. In compiling this assortment, I often found nuance, and subtleness molded into a form that provoked a smile, a laugh, and an overall good feeling. I think the authors in this collection hit the mark and can call themselves Humorists.

We would love to hear what you think about the stories told here. Please consider writing a review of the collection on Amazon. Single out the best story or stories and tell how they made you feel. That is a great way to give this collection some exposure. These are stories that you might hear in a local diner or gathering place where fun and positivity are key ingredients. If you get the feeling that the author was telling YOU the tale then our work is done. Thanks for reading. We will be doing this again.

Submissions for volume II of Heard at a UTAH Diner will be open from November 1, 2019 until March 31, 2020. Watch for details on our website humoranthology.com.

Alice M Batzel

Alice M Batzel is a Freelance Writer, Poet, Mystery & Humor Author, and Playwright with several publishing credits. Her current writing pursuits consist of a female private detective series, several contemporary clean romance novels, magazine articles, and poetry. She also writes book reviews for her website, electronic media marketing sites, and social media. Alice feels that "Laughter is the good medicine of life and we are all in need of a good dose of it as often as we can get it." She finds that real life is an abundant resource for the best humor. She makes her home with husband, Joseph in Brigham City, Utah. Learn more about Alice and her work at www.alicembatzel.com.

Stories included in this anthology:

UTAH or Bust!
Chickenpox

Betti Avari

Betti Avari lives, loves and laughs in the Rocky Mountains of Northern Utah, where nature, friends, and family play crucial roles in her life. Betti chases her interests wherever they lead, fueling her creativity with her sometimes messy, albeit curated life. Whether poolside, courtside, at a rodeo or a symphony concert, wherever you find her she'll be seeking good times, because in her opinion, "Life's too short not to!" Her eclectic experiences lend themselves to a variety of writing genres, from YA Contemporary and Middle-Grade Historical Fiction to horror, speculative, and, yes, humor. She's thankful for the endless flow of love and support from the Clandestine Writerhood Guild, the Brigham City Writers, and her husband, whose tireless attempts to imbue her with a sense of humor are very much appreciated

Stories included in this anthology:

Brigham City Sunshine and Moonshine

Cecelie Costley

Cecelie Costley writes to entertain and inspire and has published magazine and newspaper articles. She enjoys all genres and always has many works waiting for endings. She is probably most widely known for her story "The Parable of the Shopper" first published in Ideals Vol.55. The story began showing up in magazines, in religious manuals, in a Christmas anthology and even on a radio broadcast as author unknown. The story currently has a life of its own in cyberspace where Cecelie is happy to let it continue to influence others. She grew up in Salt Lake City, Utah where she married Wynn Costley. They raised seven children and now entertain twenty-eight grandchildren from time to time.

Stories included in this anthology:

Where Do You Hang Your Coat?

Dave Willes

Dave Willes is an active Blogger/Humorist deeply entrenched in Utah (although he does admit to being born in Idaho), and family. He and his wife Jana make their home in Brigham City, Utah. David's creative talents have taken him to local stage and musical productions here in Utah, including roles as Joseph, in Joseph and the Amazing Technicolor Dreamcoat, produced and directed by Rosemary Matthews, Fiddler on TheRoof as Tevye, Heritage Community Theatre, 1776 as John Adams, She Loves Me, The Fantasticks, The Sound of Music, My Fair Lady, Godspell, Saturday's Warrior, Jekyll and Hyde, Oliver.

Stories included in this anthology:

One and Done

J Audrey Hammer

J. Audrey Hammer earned a journalism degree and now uses those skills to correct grammar and punctuation in library books. After college, she eventually landed a job editing mostly un-read instructions for dentists on how to use dangerous chemicals. It also means she's now a qualified fake dentist. When not writing science fiction and fantasy, Audrey enjoys baking and decorating cakes, teaching music, and playing six instruments. (Not all at the same time. Yet.) Because that's not enough insanity, she is also the mom of five nerdy kids. After they pretend they are in bed, she enjoys re-watching episodes of "Doctor Who," "Red Dwarf," and "Buffy the Vampire Slayer." Her life's ambition is to be able to sleep in every day. Her death's ambition is to haunt bookstores in the afterlife, where there will be plenty of time to read. Because Audrey has dealt with depression for most of her life, she has developed a snarky sense of humor as a coping mechanism. You can find funny stories about everyday life at jaudreyhammer.blogspot.com or, for serious (mostly) grammar and writing tips, see audreytheeditor.blogspot.com.

Stories included in this anthology:

The Road from Grief

James D Beers

James D. Beers is an archaeologist, part-time humor, ghost story, and young adult story writer, and frequent stress eater formerly from northern Utah and now living in central Arkansas with his wife, Jenna, and son, Joseph. He loves ice cream, steak, and driving questionable two-track roads in the wilderness. His writerly side is chronicled on his website, writingwithbeers.com. He's the award-winning author of A Knack for Embarrassment (2016), Laughs & Spooks, Volume 1 (2018), Retribution (in Weird Wasatch 2018), and "Christmas Cookie . . . Ooh, la la!" (in At First Glance 2018).

Stories included in this anthology:

To Woo or Not to Woo? Dancing Begs the Question
Bee in My Bonnet
The Paddock
The Last Defiance of a Reluctant Churchgoer

Jared Quan

Jared Quan is published in genres from Spy-Thriller to Horror/Supernatural, to Fantasy-Comedy. His works include Changing Wax, Last Outpost on Zombie Highway and award-winning short story Prepped.

He served the community in key roles with the League of Utah Writers, Storymakers, Cultural Arts Society of West Jordan, EMAA, BigWorldNetwork, TEDx SaltLakeCity, UVU Book Academy, Utah Poet Laureate Selection Committee, AITP, and for countless events and organizations.

Jared has received Gold Volunteer Service Awards from the President of the United States, awards from Utah State Governor and Lt. Governor for his more than 2,000 hours of service to the writing community from 2015 to 2019.

Stories included in this anthology:

Please Don't Stop the Music

John M Olsen

John M Olsen edits and writes speculative fiction across multiple genres and loves stories about ordinary people stepping up to do extraordinary things. He hopes to entertain and inspire others with his award-winning stories as he passes his passion on to the next generation of avid readers. John has sold over twenty short stories, and loves experimenting with ideas and building skills in short format. The fast turnaround means new skills are learned more quickly. He has also released two novels, Crystal King and Crystal Queen, and will soon release the third book of that fantasy trilogy. As the President-Elect of the League of Utah Writers, he encourages others at every opportunity and hopes to see the local community produce many more great authors. Check out his ramblings on his blog. Safety goggles are optional but recommended.

johnmolsen.blogspot.com/

Stories included in this anthology:

Providence Canyon

Josie Hulme

Josie Hulme is a wife, a mother, and a writer. She grew up in Idaho and spent her childhood roaming the mountains and building her family's log house. She spent a year abroad and then joined the Marine Corps where she met her husband. They moved to Utah with two kids, where they added three more children to their family and bought a small brick house with plans to remodel. They have successfully proven the adage that you don't own a house—the house owns you. The addition spoken of in this piece is still on-going. By the middle of winter, she and her husband finally re-installed the stove, the washing machine and the kitchen sink— six months and countless man-hours later than she promised. Her husband is a saint.

Josie has won numerous awards, published several pieces, and is excited to be a part of this humorous adventure. Life is good.

Stories included in this anthology:

Raising Kids

Kathy Davidson

Kathy Davidson lives the dream high up on a hill overlooking beautiful Bear Lake with her talented husband and their large bloodhound, Rufus. She loves watching cloud formations blow across the valley, naming the ones that show up often. After raising three kids, Kathy went back to school and earned a bachelor's degree in English She's been a substitute teacher, librarian, 4-H leader, bank teller, and Post Master. She can also sew anything from wedding dresses to horse tack. Her favorite is sewing costumes, Halloween or cosplay. Now she spends her time sewing and writing with equal passion. Her novel "The House at Dietrich Hollow" is available on Amazon. "Fishing with Heber Stock" won second place in New Writer: Creative Non-Fiction 2018 category, in The League of Utah Writer's writing contest.

Stories included in this anthology:

Fishing with Heber Stock

Mike Nelson

Mike Nelson grew up on a small farm in northern Utah where he entertained himself with daydreams. A corn field could become an impenetrable jungle, a hideaway, or an enchanted forest. The hayloft in an old barn could become a pirate ship, a castle, or a frontier fort. An irrigation canal could become a raging river or a lost river of no return. Daydreams are the stuff of writing.

"Noveling" is the best Hobby he claims he has ever had. Mike currently claims authorship of three: Thorns of Avarice, Treehouse in the Hood, and Clairvoyant. My novel Clairvoyant won the League of Utah Writers Silver Quill award for Adult Fiction for 2019. Find him on Amazon.

Stories included in this anthology:

Rats

Steve Odenthal

Steve Odenthal is a Humorist, Playwright, and Publisher living in the Intermountain West. He enjoys spinning a Chimney Fishing tale or two in a humorous way. His long enduring wife, Valerie, explains these as stories of things that ALMOST went right. Together, they enjoy travel, grandkids and life. Writing is a huge passion and a couple of his Stage Plays and Humorous essays have even been enjoyed internationally. He strongly believes that humor is the common ground which will re-unite communities in today's world. He is the founder of:

humoranthology.com
playwrightsalley.com
steveodenthal.com

Steve welcomes friends on Facebook and other social media.

Stories included in this anthology:

The Grass Is Always Greener Where the Sidewalk Ends
Tenacious Monkey Bites
The Reverence Dog of Thurber Ward
Chimney Fishing in the Rockies
When the Going Gets Tough There Is Always the Window

Tyler Brian Nelson

Tyler Brian Nelson enjoys hiking, jamming along to Jack Johnson on his guitar, and trading poems with his wife. He has been writing since the first grade when he wrote an informational editorial about eagles, followed by a space epic about Mario and Luigi. Tyler attends Utah Valley University, majoring in English Education. He and his wife currently live in Provo, Utah, in a quiet little neighborhood overlooking the valley.

Stories included in this anthology:

The Bear Lake Monster

Made in the USA
Monee, IL
29 January 2020